THE CIVILIZATION OF THE AMERICAN INDIAN SERIES
(COMPLETE LIST ON PAGES 199–206)

# THE DAWES ACT
# AND THE
# ALLOTMENT
# OF INDIAN LANDS

HENRY LAURENS DAWES

# THE
# DAWES ACT
# AND THE
# ALLOTMENT
# OF
# INDIAN LANDS

BY D. S. OTIS

EDITED AND WITH AN INTRODUCTION
BY FRANCIS PAUL PRUCHA

NORMAN
UNIVERSITY OF OKLAHOMA PRESS

Library of Congress Cataloging in Publication Data
Otis, Delos Sacket, 1898–
        The Dawes act and the allotment of Indian land.
        (The Civilization of the American Indian series, v. 123)
        Originally published in 1934 in Readjustment of Indian affairs
(hearings on H. R. 7902 before the House of Representatives' Com-
mittee on Indian Affairs), pt. 9, p. 428–489, under title: History of
the allotment policy. The 1973 ed. includes corrections and minor
changes.
        Includes bibliographical references.
        1. Indians of North America—Land tenure.
I. Prucha, Francis Paul, ed. II. United States. Congress. House.
Committee on Indian Affairs. Hearings. Pt. 9, p. 428–489. 1973.
III. Title. IV. Series.
KF5660.O85        333.1'1'09701        72-3597
ISBN 0-8061-1039-2


New edition copyright 1973 by the University of Oklahoma Press,
Publishing Division of the University. Composed and printed at Norman, Oklahoma, U.S.A., by the University of Oklahoma Press. First
printing of the new edition.

*The Dawes Act and the Allotment of Indian Land* is Volume 123 in
*The Civilization of the American Indian Series.*

# CONTENTS

# EDITOR'S INTRODUCTION

The Dawes Act of February 8, 1887, providing for the allotment of Indian lands in severalty, was one of the most important pieces of legislation dealing with Indian affairs in United States history. It was the culmination of many decades of agitation for a change in Indian land tenure. Humanitarian reformers, concerned with the welfare of the Indian and anxious to speed him along the road to civilization, had always considered the private ownership of land to be an indispensable means for the acculturation of the Indians and their eventual assimilation into white society.

Henry Knox, secretary of war under Washington, hinted at individual ownership of land in a speech sent to the northwestern Indians in April, 1792. The United States, he told them, "should be greatly gratified with the opportunity of imparting to you all the blessings of civilized life, of teaching you to cultivate the earth, and raise corn; to raise oxen, sheep, and other domestic animals; to build comfortable houses, and to educate your children, so as ever to dwell upon the land." President Thomas Jefferson told a delegation of chiefs in 1808, "Let me entreat you . . . on the land now given you, to begin to give every man a farm; let him enclose it, cultivate it, build a warm house on it, and when he dies, let it belong to his wife and children after him." Secretary of War Lewis Cass in 1831 listed the adoption of severalty in property as one of the elements in fixing the "future destiny of the Indians" on a permanent basis. And the Commissioner of Indian Affairs in 1838, T. Hartley Crawford, expressed a common opinion when he wrote: "Unless some system is marked out by which there shall be a separate allotment of land to each individual . . . , you will look in vain for any general casting off of savagism. Common property and civilization cannot co-exist."

Not until the decades following the Civil War, at a time when white pressures on Indian lands brought a new crisis to Indian relations, did a concerted drive for allotment in severalty begin. To many reformers this was the most important means of destroying tribalism, and almost all of the reform groups that interested themselves in Indian affairs strongly advocated the measure. Piecemeal legislation that authorized allotment for one tribe at a time was not enough, they argued. The panacea they sought was a general allotment law, and they fought energetically for such legislation. To be sure, they met opposition. Indian groups objected to a change from traditional ways, and outspoken men like Senator Henry M. Teller of Colorado and Dr. Thomas A. Bland, editor of *The Council Fire*, vigorously fought the measure. But in the end the criticisms were brushed aside, and when success came in 1887 the majority of men concerned about Indian reform hailed the law as the "Indian Emancipation Act" and rejoiced over the "new epoch in Indian affairs." Land hungry westerners were happy, too, for the surplus lands of the reservations, over and beyond what was needed for the allotments, would be opened up

x

for their exploitation. It seemed to many that at last the end of the "Indian problem" was in sight.

D. S. Otis in this book presents both an admirably balanced account of the motives of the advocates of the allotment policy and a careful investigation of the effects of the Dawes Act up to 1900. He does not stop with the passage of the law but proceeds to study the ways in which the legislation functioned in the crucial early years after its enactment. Nor does he treat his subject in a vacuum, for he shows how the allotment policy fitted well into the dominant views of that age of individualism.

Otis researched a tremendous body of material to determine contemporary views. The reports of the Secretaries of the Interior and the Commissioners of Indian Affairs (with the voluminous reports from Indian agents that were appended each year to these official reports), the annual reports and other publications of the reform organizations that pushed so vigorously for allotment, and Congressional debates and reports form the basis of his work. The extensive footnoting not only attests to the author's diligence but offers a sure guide to others who might wish to investigate the sources. By including in his narrative numerous extracts from the documents he used, Otis conveys to the reader something of the sincerity, enthusiasm, and benevolent intentions of many of the reformers who were responsible for the Dawes Act. His study is a straightforward presentation without special literary felicity or embellishments, as was common in the monographic genre in which he wrote. Yet it is compelling and his points are strongly made. No one can read his book without gaining a clearer understanding of the motives that lay behind the Dawes Act and of the disastrous consequences of the legislation.

A graduate of Amherst College (1920), with a Ph.D. in

American history from the University of Wisconsin (1929), Otis was employed by the Bureau of Indian Affairs to write a history of allotment under the Dawes Act. His monograph, entitled "History of the Allotment Policy," was originally printed in *Readjustment of Indian Affairs* (Hearings before the Committee on Indian Affairs, House of Representatives, Seventy-third Congress, Second Session, on H. R. 7902, Washington, Government Printing Office, 1934), Part 9, pp. 428–89. The bill under discussion, introduced in the Senate by Burton K. Wheeler of Montana on February 6, 1934, and in the House by Edgar Howard of Nebraska on February 12, became law on June 18, 1934, as the Wheeler-Howard Act or Indian Reorganization Act. The bill marked a major shift in Indian policy, for it reversed the philosophy that lay behind allotment in severalty, and Commissioner of Indian Affairs John Collier, the man most responsible for the change in views, was interested in providing full information for the Committee's deliberations. Appointed by Franklin D. Roosevelt in 1933, Collier possessed a strong social science background and had served for ten years as executive secretary of the American Indian Defense Association. He was the best informed federal official on the subject of Indian policy.

Collier's proposal to include Otis's monograph in the report of the Hearings gives an interesting sidelight to the history of the monograph. He was questioned by Congressman Howard, the chairman of the Committee, and by Congressmen Fred C. Gilchrist (Republican from Iowa), Theodore B. Werner (Democrat from South Dakota), Hubert H. Peavey (Republican from Wisconsin), and William A. Ayres (Democrat from Kansas).

Mr. COLLIER . . . . There is a document which I would

like to mention, which the committee may want to have in the hearings. So much of this bill arises out of the allotment situation, and there does not exist in print anywhere an adequate record of the workings of the allotment development down the years, how it arose, how it was developed, and what it has resulted in. But, within recent months, the Indian Office has employed a competent historian, a Mr. Otis, who has made an extremely interesting resumé of the law, the history of the allotment from the beginning down to the present. It is a document of about 30,000 words, and I do not know whether the committee wants to put it in the record or not, but it would be of great value to persons interested in Indian affairs.

It has nothing to do with the bill, but it is a basic study of the history of the allotment from all of the data obtainable.

If the committee desires it, I will be glad to offer it for the record.

Mr. GILCHRIST. Why, Mr. Commissioner? You say it has nothing to do with the bill.

Mr. COLLIER. I mean, it was not prepared in connection with the bill.

Mr. GILCHRIST. My idea was that allotments had a very great deal to do with the bill.

Mr. COLLIER. They have, everything; but this document by Mr. Otis was not prepared as a part of any piece of legislation or in connection with legislation, but it was purely an attempt to get the data out of which remedies called for might be derived.

Mr. WERNER. You say that that has nothing whatever to do with the bill.

Mr. COLLIER. Anything about allotments has to do with the bill, of course.

Mr. WERNER. It would encumber the record to put that in, would it?

Mr. COLLIER. It has not been printed, and we have no immediate way of printing it, and it would be of very general interest and value to the committee, Members of Congress, and all who are interested in Indian affairs. Whether you pass this bill or not, you still have the problem of allotments on your hands.

Mr. WERNER. It is not in any sense propaganda, but is a factual compilation?

Mr. COLLIER. Yes; that is correct. I am not urging it at all, but I am sure the committee and the Members of Congress would find it useful.

Mr. GILCHRIST. I would say, aside from the consideration of this bill, as you say, a historical study of allotments would be of value to Congress, either on this bill or all of the allotment bills that are before us. It is a very important matter, I think.

The CHAIRMAN. If there is no objection, Mr. Gilchrist, the statement will be received by the committee from the Commissioner as documents of historical value and information to the committee.

Mr. PEAVEY. I would like to know if this document you refer to sets up clearly the operation of the allotment law on each reservation and in each State, so that it would not only be of value to Congress, but also the people of the States.

Mr. COLLIER. It is an attempt to show how the allotment policy arose out of the consideration of conditions then existing, and then how it evolved down to the present time, but it does not go as far as you suggest, Mr. Peavey.

Mr. AYRES. It brings up the present condition also, does it not?

Mr. COLLIER. Not in the way I have endeavored to do, because it emphatically intends not to be a political propaganda document, but contains data you gentlemen would want.

Although the chairman of the Committee was reluctant to enter the monograph into the record, he eventually directed that it be inserted in its entirety. How much use was made of it or how it affected the Committee's deliberations cannot be determined, but Collier's action saved the work for later students of the history of American Indian policy. Its value for them is without question. Anyone who wants to understand the course of Indian-white relations in the last hundred years must take into account the events and attitudes that Otis discusses.

Several books dealing with the Dawes Act, reform movements, or Indian allotments have appeared since Otis wrote his monograph. J. P Kinney's *A Continent Lost—A Civilization Won: Indian Land Tenure in America* (Baltimore, 1937) devotes half its chapters to a consideration of allotment. The book is valuable as a chronological compilation of data dealing with the whole allotment question, but it offers little analysis or interpretation and lacks the force of Otis's presentation. Loring Benson Priest's *Uncle Sam's Stepchildren: The Reformation of United States Indian Policy, 1865–1887* (New Brunswick, New Jersey, 1942) treats in detail the formulation of Indian policy in the two decades before the passage of the Dawes Act, which the author considers the culmination of the Indian reform movement. But the book ends with the Dawes Act and has no parallel to Otis's careful study of the carrying out of allotment in the years following the enactment of the law. Henry E. Fritz's *The Movement for Indian Assimilation, 1860–1890* (Philadelphia, 1963) discusses the antecedents of severalty legislation and suggests that Dawes acted partly from reasons of political expediency in sponsoring the act. Robert Winston Mardock's *The Reformers and the American Indian* (Columbia, Missouri, 1971) emphasizes the reformers of the immediate post-Civil War years and gives little attention to the Dawes Act. None of these authors appears to have used Otis's work. Nor do general studies such as William T. Hagan's *American Indians* (Chicago, 1961) and Angie Debo's *A History of the Indians of the United States* (Norman, 1970) mention its existence.

The monograph as printed in the Hearings is not readily available, nor is it in a form conducive to easy use by present-day readers. The print is small, the typographical errors are numerous, and the footnote citations are not always in convenient form. I have undertaken, therefore, with the author's permission, to make a number of changes. I have changed the title from "History of the Allotment Policy" to "The Dawes Act and the Allotment of Indian Lands," both to indicate more precisely the nature of the work and to call attention to the Dawes Act, which is the focus of the study. The sections of the monograph have been used as chapters, with the original titles, except for the two short initial sections, which have been combined under a new title to form Chapter I. Long quotations, which in the original were uniformly run into the text, have been set in blocked form for easier identification. All the direct quotations have been checked against the original printed sources, and changes that were made when the monograph was published in the Hearings have been corrected. Consistent usage in punctuation and capitalization has been adopted, and full names have been supplied for persons mentioned in the book when they first occur.

Otis did the bulk of his research in the Indian Office library, and many of his footnote citations refer to material assembled there in bound volumes of miscellaneous documents. I have changed these footnotes to standard citations of the material used. For the sake of uniformity and to indicate more clearly the work of members of the Lake Mohonk Conferences, reference is made to the separately published *Proceedings* of the Conferences rather than to the printing of the same material in the annual reports of the Board of Indian Commissioners, to which the original notes often refer. In a few cases I have combined footnotes when they refer to the same source. References to the *United States Statutes at Large*, which Otis entered in the text itself, have been dropped to the footnotes. Whereas the notes in the original were numbered in sequence through the entire monograph, there is now a new series of notes for each chapter.

These changes are technical only and were made for the convenience of the reader. They do not affect the text of the monograph, which appears here in its original form except for a few corrections in dates, persons cited, or similar factual information which the rechecking of the sources suggested. The index has been supplied by the editor.

FRANCIS PAUL PRUCHA, S.J.

*Marquette University*
*December, 1972*

# THE DAWES ACT
# AND THE
# ALLOTMENT
# OF INDIAN LANDS

# CHAPTER I

## THE GENERAL ALLOTMENT LAW
## (DAWES ACT)

In the 1870's the Government's policy of general allotment of Indian lands in severalty gradually took form. The idea of allotment had, in theory and practice, previously been known. Perhaps the first proposal of this sort is to be found in a report of Secretary of War William H. Crawford to President James Madison in 1816.[1] In the Choctaw Treaty of 1805 the Government had begun the practice of reserving for individuals certain tracts of land for which patents in many cases were issued later.[2] At any rate, in an act providing for the distribution of the Brotherton Indians' lands Congress in 1839 expressly used the term "allotment."[3] By 1885 the Government had, under various treaties and laws, issued over 11,000 patents to individual Indians and 1,290 certificates of allotment.[4] The fact that 8,595 of these patents and 1,195 of these certificates were issued under laws passed and treaties ratified during the period 1850–1869 suggests that the forces which produced the General Allotment Act of 1887 were coming to life in the mid-century. In 1862 Congress saw fit to pass a law for the special protection of the Indian allottee in the enjoyment and use of his land.[5] And in 1875 Congress gave

further momentum to the whole lands-in-severalty movement by extending to the Indian homesteading privileges.[6]

In the meantime the Indian Administration was gravi-
tating steadily to the position of supporting allotment as a
general principle. In 1870 the Commissioner of Indian Affairs noted that Indians were increasingly demanding allotments, and he thought that the policy of "giving to every
Indian a home that he can call his own" was a wise one.
He recommended "the adoption, generally, of this plan."
The following year he again expressed his interest in an extension of the allotment scheme.[7] In 1872 the new Commissioner, Francis A. Walker, avoided all reference to the
question, but he attacked the idea of citizenship for the
Indian as pernicious, and it is probable that he was opposed
to allotment as well.[8] The next Commissioner in his report
for 1873 spoke out emphatically in favor of a general allotment law.[9] Thereafter, with few exceptions, the annual
reports advocated general legislation, the Commissioner in
1876 going so far as to ask for a law "not only permitting,
but requiring, the head of each Indian family, to accept the
allotment of a reasonable amount of land." He wrote, "It
is doubtful whether any high degree of civilization is possible without individual ownership of land."[10] The Secretaries of the Interior responded more slowly to the idea—
at least so far as official recommendations were concerned.
Secretary Columbus Delano in 1874 had urged the adoption
of homestead legislation, and the next year Secretary Zacha-
riah Chandler noted that "the desire of the Indians to prepare for themselves more comfortable and fixed abodes" was
"becoming more general."[11]

In his next annual report he pointed out that the Commissioner of Indian Affairs had asked for a comprehensive
allotment law.[12] In 1877 Secretary Carl Schurz recom-

mended allotment to heads of families on all reservations, "the enjoyment and pride of the individual ownership of property being one of the most effective civilizing agencies."[13] From that date onward the Service as a whole worked for the speeding up of allotment under previous acts and treaties and the passage of a general law. In 1876 the Commissioner wrote, "I am not unaware that this proposition will meet with strenuous opposition from the Indians themselves. Like the whites, they have ambitious men, who will resist to the utmost of their power any change tending to reduce the authority which they have acquired by personal effort or by inheritance."[14] But in 1879 Secretary Schurz reported, "The desire for allotment of lands in severalty is now expressed by Indians on a considerable number of reservations with great urgency."[15] Apparently the Indian agents were doing their best. In 1883 the Fond du Lac agent wrote that his Indians had been hostile to the idea of allotment but that since his visits to them they had "become desirous to select allotments" and seemed "deeply interested in the school."[16] In 1886 the Commissioner announced a policy of instructing agents to urge allotment upon the Indians in every possible case.[17]

In the late seventies there was a growing public opinion in support of the allotment movement. The Commissioner in 1880 declared, "It [allotment] is a measure correspondent with the progressive age in which we live, and is indorsed by all true friends of the Indian, as is evidenced by the numerous petitions to this effect presented to Congress from citizens of various States."[18]

Early in 1879 a joint committee of Congress, appointed to consider the matter of transferring the Indian Bureau to the War Department, reported a decision adverse to the change and proceeded to make recommendations of measures to civilize the Indians. One of their proposals was a general allotment law providing for a title in fee with a twenty-five-year restriction upon alienation.[19] The same day, January 31, 1879, Chairman Alfred M. Scales of the House Committee on Indian Affairs reported a general allotment bill.[20] In the next Congress various bills were introduced to the same effect.[21] The House committee on May 28, 1880, reported favorably an allotment bill and accompanied it with statements of the majority and minority views.[22] In the Senate the measure which was to be known for the next few years as the "Coke bill" was introduced.[23] Senator Henry L. Dawes in 1885 credited Carl Schurz with having originated the bill.[24] Its provisions were substantially the same as those of the ultimate Dawes Act, except that the Indian was not thereby declared a citizen.[25] The Coke bill passed the Senate in 1884 and in 1885 and in this latter year was favorably reported in the House.[26] In the meantime certain tribes by special laws were given the privilege of allotments in severalty—the Crows on April 11, 1882, the Omahas on August 7, 1882, and the Umatillas on March 3, 1885.[27] These acts applied to specific reservations the principles of the Coke bill.

The allotment movement seemed rapidly to be gaining strength in 1886. President Grover Cleveland in his annual messages in 1885 and 1886 advocated the policy.[28] In 1886 General Philip H. Sheridan, reporting as Lieutenant General of the Army to the Secretary of War, likewise urged an allotment scheme.[29] Finally, Congress acted early in the following year, and the President signed the Dawes Act on February 8, 1887.[30] The chief provisions of the act were: (1) a grant of 160 acres to each family head, of eighty acres to each single person over eighteen years of age and to each orphan under eighteen, and of forty acres to each other single person under eighteen; (2) a patent in fee to be issued to every allottee but to be held in trust by the Government for twenty-five years, during which time the land could not be alienated or encumbered; (3) a period of four years to be allowed the Indians in which they should make their selections after allotment should be applied to any tribe—failure of the Indians to do so should result in selection for them at the order of the Secretary of the Interior; (4) citizenship to be conferred upon allottees and upon any other Indians who had abandoned their tribes and adopted "the habits of civilized life."[31] So the Indian was to become an independent farmer and a citizen of the Republic.

# CHAPTER II

## AIMS AND MOTIVES
## OF THE ALLOTMENT MOVEMENT

That the leading proponents of allotment were inspired by the highest motives seems conclusively true. A Member of Congress, speaking on the Dawes bill in 1886, said, "It has . . . the indorsement of the Indian rights associations throughout the country, and of the best sentiment of the land."[1] The new policy was regarded as a panacea which would make restitution to the Indian for all that the white man had done to him in the past. Senator Dawes told the Mohonk Conference in 1885:

> I feel just this; that every dollar of money, and every hour of effort that can be applied to each individual Indian, day and night, in season and out of season, with patience and perseverance, with kindness and with charity, is not only due him in atonement for what we have inflicted upon him in the past, but is our own obligation towards him in order that we may not have him a vagabond and a pauper, without home or occupation among us in this land.[2]

The supreme aim of the friends of the Indian was to substitute white civilization for his tribal culture, and they shrewdly sensed that the difference in the concepts of property was fundamental to the contrast between the two ways of life. That the white man's way was good and the Indian's way was bad, all agreed. So, on the one hand, allotment was counted on to break up tribal life. This blessing was dwelt upon at length. The agent for the Yankton Sioux wrote in 1877:

> As long as Indians live in villages they will retain many of their old and injurious habits. Frequent feasts, community in food, heathen ceremonies and dances, constant visiting—these will continue as long as the people live together in close neighborhoods and villages. . . . I trust that before another year is ended they will generally be located upon individual lands of farms. From that date will begin their real and permanent progress.[3]

On the other hand, the allotment system was to enable the Indian to acquire the benefits of civilization. The Indian agents of the period made no effort to conceal their disgust for tribal economy. One of them wrote in 1882: "The allotment of land in severalty will go a long way, in my judgment, towards making these more advanced tribes still nearer the happy goal. I do not think that the results of labor ought to be evenly distributed irrespective of the merits of individuals, for that would discourage effort; but under the present communistic state of affairs such would appear to be the result of the labor of many."[4]

Supporters of allotment showed themselves children of their age in their deference to the principle of individualism. In 1873 the Commissioner of Indian Affairs wrote, "A fundamental difference between barbarians and a civilized people is the difference between a herd and an individual."[5] During the discussion of the new policy at the third Lake Mohonk Conference in 1885, John H. Oberly, Superintendent of Indian Schools and subsequently, for a few months,

Commissioner of Indian Affairs, went about as far as one could go in resolving the American society into its individual units. He said:

> "We, the people," was the reply the Americans made to the King, by which answer every man who was devoted to the cause of independence said: "I, the individual, agreeing with my fellow citizens in this conclusion;—I, the individual, having an inalienable right to life, liberty, and the pursuit of happiness, unite with other individuals in saying that the answer to the heretofore unanswered riddle of statesmanship is Man, for whom all governments should be created, because from the individual all legitimate political power primarily flows." (Applause.)[6]

The Indian, then, was to learn to go his own independent, industrious way and he would become civilized. Probably most citizens in 1881 would have applauded Senator George H. Pendleton when in debating the Coke bill he invoked the American law and prophets. He said, "It must be our part to seek to foster and to encourage within them [the Indians] this trinity upon which all civilization depends—family, and home, and property."[7] One cannot but wonder how many would have subscribed to the astounding utterances of Senator Dawes, himself, in an address to the 1885 Lake Mohonk Conference:

> The head chief told us that there was not a family in that whole Nation [one of the Five Civilized Tribes] that had not a home of its own. There was not a pauper in that Nation, and the Nation did not owe a dollar. It built its own capitol . . . and it built its schools and its hospitals. Yet the defect of the system was apparent. They have got as far as they can go, because they own their land in common. It is Henry George's system, and under

that there is no enterprise to make your home any better than that of your neighbors. There is no selfishness, which is at the bottom of civilization. Till this people will consent to give up their lands, and divide them among their citizens so that each can own the land he cultivates, they will not make much more progress.[8]

But voices of doubt were here and there raised about allotment as a wholesale civilizing program. "Barbarism" was not without its defenders. Especially were the Five Civilized Tribes held up as an example of felicity under a communal system in contrast to the deplorable condition of certain Indians upon whom allotment had been tried.[9] A minority report of the House Committee on Indian Affairs in 1880 went so far as to state that Indians had made progress only under communism.[10] At this point it is worth remarking that friends and enemies of allotment alike showed no clear understanding of Indian agricultural economy. Both were prone to use the word "communism" in a loose sense in describing Indian enterprise. It was in the main an inaccurate term. General O. O. Howard told the Lake Mohonk Conference in 1889 about a band of Spokane Indians who worked their lands in common in the latter part of the 1870's,[11] but certainly in the vast majority of cases Indian economic pursuits were carried on directly with individual rewards in view. This was primarily true even of such essentially group activities as the Omahas' annual buffalo hunt.[12] Agriculture was certainly but rarely a communal undertaking. The Pueblos, who had probably the oldest and most established agricultural economy, were individualistic in farming and pooled their efforts only in the care of the irrigation system.[13] What the allotment debaters meant by communism was that the title to land invariably rested in the tribe and the actual holding of the land was dependent

11

on its use and occupancy. They also meant vaguely the co-operativeness and clannishness—the strong communal sense—of barbaric life, which allotment was calculated to disrupt.

In any event, the doubters were skeptical as to whether this allotment method of civilizing would work. They placed much emphasis upon the fact that Indian life was bound up with the communal holding of land. In 1881 Senator Henry M. Teller quoted a chief's explanation why the Nez Perces went on the warpath: "They asked us to divide the land, to divide our mother upon whose bosom we had been born, upon whose lap we had been reared."[14] In the same debate Senator John T. Morgan said, "The communal institution . . . [of Russia] is almost indistinguishable from the system of the Indians. These people understand from experience what is better for them than we understand with all our knowledge."[15] Senator Teller spoke with high scorn of the exalted dreams of allotment advocates: "I know it will be said, 'Why, in twenty-five years they will all be civilized; these people will be church-going farmers, having schools and all the appliances of civilized life in twenty-five years.' " He proceeded to show that early in the century Jedidiah Morse expected the complete civilization of the Indians in twenty years.[16] The minority of the House Committee on Indian Affairs doubted whether private property would transform the Indian. The minority report said:

> However much we may differ with the humanitarians who are riding this hobby, we are certain that they will agree with us in the proposition that it does not make a farmer out of an Indian to give him a quarter-section of land. There are hundreds of thousands of white men, rich with the experiences of centuries of Anglo-Saxon civilization, who cannot be transformed into cultivators of the land by any such gift.[17]

The believers in allotment had another philanthropic aim, which was to protect the Indian in his present land holding. They were confident that if every Indian had his own strip of land, guaranteed by a patent from the Government, he would enjoy a security which no tribal possession could afford him. If the Indian's possession was further safeguarded by a restriction upon his right to sell it, they believed that the system would be foolproof. The friends of the Indians were here dealing with the fundamental problem of the relations of the two races. The age-old process of dispossessing the Indian was in this period rapidly accelerating. The railroads were giving powerful impetus to the westward march of land-hungry native Americans and even more voracious European immigrants, whose number was daily increasing. Furthermore, the new industrial needs made mining and lumbering operations far more—and the Indian's title to his land far less—important. In 1881 Carl Schurz wrote, "There is nothing more dangerous to an Indian reservation than a rich mine. But the repeated invasions of the Indian Territory, as well as many other similar occurrences, have shown clearly enough that the attraction of good agricultural lands is apt to have the same effect, expecially when great railroad enterprises are pushing in the same direction."[18] And it was allotment he looked to to stem these tides.

The Government itself, when political pressure became strong, had not always shown the will to refrain from disturbing Indian rights. In 1884 a speaker at the Lake Mohonk Conference said, "... by our refusal to protect them in the possession of their land, and by our incessant removals we take away the common motives for cultivating it."[19]

When fifty-five Omaha Indians petitioned Congress for an allotment of their lands in severalty in 1882, they were remembering the fact that their kindred, the Poncas, had in 1877 been uprooted by the Government and transplanted to the "hot country." Statements from most of the fifty-five Omahas accompanied the memorial to Congress and invariably explained that the petitioners wanted titles to their lands so that they might feel secure in their holdings.[20] But is was clear that the aggressor and the menace to Indian property rights was not directly the Government but the white settler and promoter. At the Lake Mohonk Conference in 1887 much was said about the breaking down of reservations, in the interest of civilizing the Indian. Senator Dawes rose to remark: "You talk about the necessity of doing away with the reservation system; a power that you can never resist has broken it up into homesteads, has taken possession of it, has driven the game from out of it . . . . Something stronger than the Mohonk Conference has dissolved the reservation system. The greed of these people for the land has made it utterly impossible to preserve it for the Indian."[21] Indeed the power to which the Senator referred was proving itself not only stronger than the Lake Mohonk Conference but stronger than the Government itself. There is ample evidence to indicate that officials at times turned to the allotment program as a means of salvaging for the Indian a fraction of that whole property interest which the Government could no longer protect. Carl Schurz, writing in 1881, told how when feeling against the Utes was running high in Colorado, where the Indians were guilty of owning valuable mining lands, the Government persuaded the Utes to accept allotments and cede the balance of their reservation save for "small tracts of agricultural and grazing lands."[22] The writer commented as follows:

It must be kept in mind that the settlement of the

Indians in severalty is one of those things for which the Indians and the Government are not always permitted to choose their own time . . . . Nobody will pretend that the Utes were fully prepared for such a change in their condition . . . . But nothing short of it would have saved the Ute tribe from destruction, and averted a most bloody and expensive conflict. . . .

The question is, whether the Indians are to be exposed to the danger of hostile collisions, and of being robbed of their lands in consequence, or whether they are to be induced by proper and fair means to sell that which, as long as they keep it, is of no advantage to anybody, but which, as soon as they part with it for a just compensation, will be a great advantage to themselves and their white neighbors alike.[23]

Implicit in this statement of Carl Schurz's is a summary of the whole Indian problem so far as Government policies are concerned. Clear is the sense of limitation and of justification. It makes understandable the entire subsequent working out of the allotment program. It was apparent that the Indian system was being smashed by the white economy and culture. Friends of the Indian, therefore, saw his one chance for survival in his adapting himself to the white civilization. He must be taught industry and acquisitiveness to fit him for his "ultimate absorption in the great body of American citizenship."[24] Making him a citizen and a voter would guarantee to him the protection of the rules under which the competitive game of life was played. And it was to be hoped that he would take his place among the more skillful white players.

In passing it seems worthwhile to suggest the relationship of this philanthropic interest in the Indian to the similar interest in the Negro. In both cases the attitudes are part

of the same general ideology. The Negro had been granted
freedom, citizenship, and suffrage. The experiment had
been by no means a complete success, yet as a Boston representative at the Lake Mohonk Conference said in 1886, "It
was argued that it would be unsafe, that it might wreck the
Republic to give to the ignorant freedman, just emanci-
pated from slavery, the rights of citizenship. But I doubt if
there is a large number of people in this broad land to-day
who do not recognize that the negroes, if they had been
kept under guardianship and not given the inspirations
which citizenship gives, would have been in a far worse
condition to-day than they are."[25] There were important
differences in the economic situations of the Negroes and
of the Indians. Yet the ideas which Booker T. Washington
was evolving with reference to the material progress of the
Negro (and which had enthusiastic support of white philanthropy) had much in common with the theories involved in allotment to the Indians. It was fitting that in
this period Hampton Institute should be a training school
for the young people of both subordinate races.

It must also be noted that while the advocates of allotment were primarily and sincerely concerned with the advancement of the Indian they at the same time regarded the
scheme as promoting the best interests of the whites as well.
For one thing, it was fondly but erroneously hoped that setting the Indian on his own feet would relieve the Government of a great expense. In 1879 the Indian Commissioner,
in recommending an allotment bill to Secretary Schurz,
wrote, "The evidently growing feeling in the country
against the continued appropriations for the care and support of the Indians indicates the necessity for a radical
change of policy in affairs connected with their lands."[26]
Speaking in favor of the Dawes bill, a Member of Congress

16

said in 1886, "What shall be his future status? Shall he remain a pauper savage, blocking the pathway of civilization,
an increasing burden upon the people? Or shall he be con-
verted into a civilized taxpayer, contributing toward the
support of the Government and adding to the material
prosperity of the country? . . . . We desire, I say, that the
latter shall be his destiny."[27]

The chief advantages that the new system was to bring
to the country as a whole were to be found in the opening
up of surplus lands on the reservations and in the attendant
march of progress and civilization westward. In his report
of 1880, Secretary Schurz wrote:

> [Allotment] will eventually open to settlement by
> white men the large tracts of land now belonging to the
> reservations, but not used by the Indians. It will thus put
> the relations between the Indians and their white neigh-
> bors in the western country upon a new basis, by grad-
> ually doing away with the system of large reservations,
> which has so frequently provoked those encroachments
> which in the past have led to so much cruel injustice and
> so many disastrous collisions.[28]

So the Indian and the white man were to profit together
from the pacification of the border, but furthermore the
Indian was to learn valuable lessons from his white neighbors. This sentiment was frequently repeated. An Indian
agent wrote in 1885 that the land when opened "would soon
be taken up, and these settlers would at once begin to open
farms, and to set an example of thrift and self-support by
the side of their Indian neighbors."[29]

There were also frequent allusions to the fact that the
Indians were of course making no use of natural resources
which should be developed in the interests of civilization.
In 1880 the Commissioner recommended the removal of

the Chippewas from their lands in Dakota and in Minnesota and a consolidation of them on the White Earth Reservation, where they were to be allotted lands in severalty. He noted that the present Chippewa lands were unfit for farming but were "chiefly valuable for the pine timber growing thereon, for which, if the Indian title should be extinguished, a ready sale could be found."[30]

It must be reported that the using of these lands which the Indians did not "need" for the advancement of civilization was a logical part of a whole and sincerely idealistic philosophy. The civilizing policy was in the long run to benefit Indian and white man alike. But doubters of the allotment system could see nothing in the policy but dire consequences for the Indian. Senator Teller in 1881 called the Coke bill "a bill to despoil the Indians of their lands and to make them vagabonds on the face of the earth."[31] At another time he said:

> If I stand alone in the Senate, I want to put upon the record my prophecy in this matter, that when thirty or forty years shall have passed and these Indians shall have parted with their title, they will curse the hand that was raised professedly in their defense to secure this kind of legislation and if the people who are clamoring for it understood Indian character, and Indian laws, and Indian morals, and Indian religion, they would not be here clamoring for this at all.[32]

In the debate on the Dawes bill in 1886 Senator Preston B. Plumb asked why, if the Five Tribes were so advanced in civilization, they should be exempted from the measure and allotment applied only to the more backward Indians. He said, ". . . to pick them out and say to them, 'root, hog, or die,' with the certainty that it will be 'die,' seems to me to be a refinement of cruelty which I would hardly have expected of my friend from Massachusetts."[33] Senator Teller had charged that allotment was in the interests of the land-grabbing speculators,[34] but the minority report of the House Indian Affairs Committee in 1880 had gone even further in its accusations. It said:

The real aim of this bill is to get at the Indian lands and open them up to settlement. The provisions for the apparent benefit of the Indian are but the pretext to get at his lands and occupy them . . . . If this were done in the name of Greed, it would be bad enough; but to do it in the name of Humanity, and under the cloak of an ardent desire to promote the Indian's welfare by making him like ourselves, whether he will or not, is infinitely worse.[35]

This statement is hardly fair to all the supporters of the allotment policy. As has been said, it is true that even the genuine friends of the Indian favored opening up his "surplus" lands in the interest of spreading civilization. But there is no doubt that they believed that the allotment policy would promote the Indian's economic and spiritual welfare. This belief was an integral part of the whole American philosophy of freedom, individualism, opportunity, and progress. However, it must be said that the allotment theory was by no means conceived in a vacuum by detached philosophers who spontaneously conceived a notion for improving the lot of the Indian. The friends of the Indian were faced with a desperate situation and an immediate problem to be solved. The expansion of the white civilization was in the process of breaking down the reservations, laws and treaties to the contrary notwithstanding. The decade of the 1880's saw the "passing of the frontier." Before the end of that decade the last of the more desirable homesteads had been taken up and the pressure of white population and enterprise was cracking the barriers around the Indian lands.[36] So, confronted by this dilemma, the friends of the Indian looked to allotment and patents in fee as means of giving to the Indian sufficient but, above all, secure lands. Senator Dawes had emphasized this point. And before him, Secretary Schurz had said that allotment was a policy for which the Government could not choose its own time.

It is probably true that the most powerful force motivating the allotment policy was the pressure of the land-hungry western settlers. A very able prize thesis written at Harvard by Samuel Taylor puts forth this theory. The author copiously and convincingly cites evidence to show the cupidity of the westerners for the Indian's lands and their unrestrained zeal in acquiring them. The author describes the situation in Colorado, where the violent actions of the white population, which Secretary Schurz noted, gave rise to the agreement reducing the Ute Reservation and allotting the Indian lands in severalty. The author also describes the illegal invasion of Indian Territory by the "boomers" and their ensuing struggle with the cattle interests that had leased the Indian lands with the tacit consent of the Government. The account further shows how the general desire of homesteaders for lands, challenged by the cattlemen who already had established through leases a monopolistic control, led to a popular demand in the West for a breaking down of the reservations. This demand was translated, especially among eastern philanthropists, into the allotment proposal as a compromise between East and West.[37]

It is difficult to prove with finality the part played by the western land seekers in the development of the allotment program. Selfish ambitions promoting legislation are never so desirous of expression as are philanthropic interests. It is the latter that provide the themes for oration and debate. But the main facts of this history are that there were powerful social and economic forces breaking down the reservations, and allotment was the legal method by means of which it was finally accomplished. A comprehensive study of western newspapers and local chronicles of this period might throw considerable light upon the problem of the motives behind allotment.

Public administrators initiated the allotment policy but it seems clear that they had in mind the demands of the westerners and the exigencies of the situation as well as the Indian's needs. The eastern philanthropists also saw allotment as a solution of the immediate problem, and they found it consistent with their ideas of progress and Christianity. As Taylor points out, the westerners would have preferred to take all of the Indian lands, but, as it was, they accepted allotment as an attainable compromise.[38] And the West seems generally to have adopted allotment. It is significant that there was no organized opposition of western Members of Congress to the Dawes bill.[39] Indeed, in the bill's later stages there was little opposition at all. And the Territorial Legislature of Dakota and the Pierre board of trade memorialized Congress in favor of the Sioux bill which became law in 1888.[40]

There were, however, clear cases of specific private interests supporting allotment for private ends—as a technique for acquiring Indian lands. In New York State the Ogden Land Company had a claim to the lands of the Senecas, which claim, however, was subject to the right of the Indians to live on the land as a tribe. In 1886 the company was trying to push an allotment bill through the New York legislature. In 1887 a speaker said to a conference

21

of friends of the Indian, ". . . the moment that the Seneca Indians part with the possession of those lands . . . or the moment their tribal relation is dissolved, the title of the Ogden Land Company becomes perfect, and Congress cannot prevent it. You have got to keep them upon that land, you have got to keep them in a tribal condition, or you must turn them over to robbers."[41] A study of the activities of lumber interests in connection with the allotment policy might prove very instructive. The technique of a "lumber ring" working with a faction in an Indian tribe to secure a special allotment law was revealed at a Mohonk Conference. Professor Charles C. Painter, national lobbyist for the Indian Rights Association, told how an allotment act for the Stockbridge and Munsee Indians in Wisconsin was rushed through Congress in 1871 and adapted to the uses of the lumber ring. Several different special agents investigated the situation and denounced the whole transaction, to no effect so far as official action was concerned. Professor Painter wrote:

There is evidence to show that the same interests (pine on the part of the white men, and power and pelf on the part of the favored Indians) which secured the act of 1871 have been able to suppress, or turn aside, the recommendations of special agents who have examined into and reported the facts and asked that the wrongs inflicted by an allotment under this act should be righted.[42]

A special enterprise which undoubtedly affected the establishing and working out of the allotment program was the railroads. It must again be remembered that the 1880's were a time of feverish railroad building. Construction went forward until in 1890 the number of miles of track per capita reached a figure which has hardly been exceeded since.[43] Fate seems never to have been more ironic than in the

tricks it played upon the Government in its policy of settling the Indians in "permanent" abodes. From the time
of Monroe's "Indian frontier" in 1825 to the final locating
of Indians on what eventually proved to be rich oil lands
in Oklahoma the Indians were forever being placed where
they would sometime get in the way of important white
enterprise.[44] In the 1880's the irrepressible railroads found
Indian reservations blocking their paths. Corporations
found the Indians not at all interested in furthering railroad progress by stepping aside, and the Government quickly felt the pressure.

Railroad activities on reservations and the Indians' re-
actions were frequently chronicled in Indian agents' reports
in the early part of the decade. In 1883 the agent of the
Fort Berthold Reservation, in Dakota, wrote that his
charges were anxious for titles to their lands, since they were
still smarting from the fact that the Government, in order
to fulfill a grant to the Northern Pacific, had taken over
half their reservation and offered them in recompense a
much smaller tract of land which was "rough and unde-
sirable." He said, "It is difficult to reconcile them, as they
fully believe that because they are weak the Government
has taken advantage of them and dealt unjustly with them.
They often assert that the white man's government would
not dare to treat the more powerful and war-like Sioux in
such manner . . . . I am constrained to confess that I am
unable to answer these complainings, which seem to be
well taken, in a satisfactory manner to myself or to the
Indians."[45]

The writer has been unable to discover any explicit expression of a railroad's attitude toward the passage of the
general allotment act. He believes that it is a subject well
worth exploring, when time permits. It is interesting that

the same session of the same Congress that passed the Dawes Act went in for grants of railroad rights-of-way through Indian lands on a new and enlarged scale. Of nine Indian bills that became law, six were railroad grants.[46] Of the remaining three, one was the Dawes Act, one was the appropriation act, and the third was an amendment to the land-sales law. In September, 1887, the Indian Commissioner remarked in his report, "The past year has been one of unusual activity in the projection and building of numerous additional railroads through Indian lands. The wisdom of Congress in granting such charters to railroad companies will, I believe, be demonstrated by the benefits to the Indian which will eventually result therefrom."[47] In 1885 the Commissioner had reported, "As to railroads affecting Indian reservations there is but little of general interest to record."[48] In the first session of the Fiftieth Congress—the session following that in which the Dawes Act was passed—thirteen laws were passed granting rights-of-way to railroads through Indian territories.[49] Although the second session of the Fiftieth Congress was the short session, it succeeded in putting ten such laws on the statute books.[50] It is at least interesting circumstantial evidence that Section 10 of the Dawes Act reads:

> That nothing in this act contained shall be so construed as to affect the right and power of Congress to grant the right-of-way through any lands granted to an Indian, or a tribe of Indians, for railroads or other highways, or telegraph lines, for the public use, or to condemn such lands to public uses, upon making just compensation.[51]

On the other hand, it has been suggested that the railroads might have been actually opposed to the allotment scheme as a policy which might render inviolate Indian titles in inconvenient places. It has also been suggested that the wholesale granting of rights-of-way in the Forty-ninth and Fiftieth Congresses may have been the product of the railroads' hustling activity to get under the bars before allotment took effect. It is true that these grants to railroads in 1887–1889 could not have come as direct benefits of the Dawes Act, since it took two or three years to work out and apply allotment on any one reservation. It is quite possible that railroads worked anxiously to get rights-of-way established before Indians were located with inalienable titles on lands which might lie in the path of railroad extension. Yet it is to be noted that subsequently, through the nineties, the railroads seemed to find no difficulty in securing grants from Congress. After a lull in 1891 and 1892, railroad legislation affecting Indian lands took a new lease on life and reached its zenith with fifteen rights-of-way grants or extensions of grants in 1898.[52] It is, of course, a doubtful question how much this legislation was actually affected by Indian land policies and how much it was but the result of more fundamental economic forces. However, regarding the interest of railroads in allotment, one salient fact that must be borne in mind is that the allotment system would throw open large areas to white settlement, and in this period especially railroad leaders were lavishly expending money and effort in building up western settlements to furnish railroad traffic.

It is significant that one of the foremost of these empire builders was discovering that under the old reservation system the way of the railroader was hard. The biographer of James J. Hill tells of the difficulties which the builder of the St. Paul, Minneapolis & Manitoba Railroad experienced in securing a right-of-way across the Fort Berthold and Blackfeet Reservations in 1886 and 1887.[53] Eventually the railroad got its grant, but the way was paved for acquiring more easily a second grant, extending the right-of-way westward, by the Blackfeet agreement of 1888.[54] This agreement cut the reservation up into several smaller ones (art. I), allowed the sale of the surplus land, provided for allotment in severalty (art. VI), and stipulated that rights-of-way might be granted through any of the separate reservations "whenever in the opinion of the President the public interests require the construction of railroads, or other highways, or telegraph lines . . ." (art. VIII). Again, the writer has no evidence to show that the railroad was active in promoting this agreement. But a later comment of James J. Hill indicates that he had been well aware of the disadvantages of the old reservations for railroading. He said:

> When we built into northern Montana, and I want to tell you that it took faith to do it, from the eastern boundary of the state to Fort Benton was unceded Indian land; no white man had a right to put two logs one on top of the other. If he undertook to remain too long in passing through the country, he was told to move on. Even when cattle crossed the Missouri River during the first years to come to our trains, the Indians asked $50 a head for walking across the land a distance of three miles, and they wanted an additional amount per head, I don't remember what it was, for the water they drank in crossing the Missouri.[55]

At any rate, a number of studies might profitably be made of railroad and allotment activities on particular reservations. The annual reports of the Commissioner of Indian Affairs contain a good deal of factual material concerning negotiations of railroads with Indians in regard to rights-of-way, attitudes of Indians, congressional grants, and the specific application of allotments. Such studies might yield only further circumstantial evidence, but at least they would contribute to the drawing of the general picture. It seems probable that there was more haste than wisdom shown in the extensive railroad legislation of this period. Of the thirteen grants of rights-of-way made by the first session of the Fiftieth Congress, President Cleveland allowed five to become law without his signature, and in his fourth annual message in 1888 he said, ". . . grants of doubtful expediency to railroad corporations, permitting them to pass through Indian reservations, have greatly multiplied."[56] There is at least one recorded instance when a railroad was not above bringing pressure upon the Government in the matter of Indian lands in general. Robert M. LaFollette was beginning his political career in 1885 in the House of Representatives. Assigned to the Committee on Indian Affairs at the outset, he gave his attention to pending bills granting rights-of-way through the Sioux country to the Chicago, Milwaukee & St. Paul and the Chicago & Northwestern railroad companies. He at once concluded that the grants were excessively large. When he voiced his opposition in committee a colleague whispered, "Bob, you don't want to interfere with that provision. *Those are your home corporations.*" But the young man persisted and one of the Senators from his State found it expedient to send for the secretary of the Wisconsin State Republican Committee, who was also lobbyist for the Chicago, Milwaukee & St. Paul road. This man, who was Henry C. Payne, told another Wisconsin Congressman, "LaFollette is a crank; if he thinks he can buck a railroad company with 5,000 miles of line, he'll find out his mistake. We'll take care of him when the time comes."[57]

As has been indicated, the writer has discovered no direct evidence of a railroad policy in regard to the allotment movement. What seems to appear is the fact that the railroads were interested in any technique of securing lands for their extension and support. There is at least the testimony of one man that a railroad on one occasion opposed the issuing of patents to the Indians to safeguard their holdings in severalty. In 1886 an agent in Washington Territory reported to the Indian Office that patents had been issued to the Puyallup Indians. He said, "Strong opposition was made by the railroad and land companies interested to the granting of these patents, and great credit is due to the administration for its fearless and efficient protection of their rights."[58] However, the granting of secure titles to Indians already holding lands in severalty and a general allotment policy which would throw open to white acquisition large areas of surplus tribal lands would be two quite different things so far as the railroads' interests were concerned.

The friends of the Indian, at least, saw a connection between allotment and railroad progress. Their attitudes seem anomalous today, yet they sprang directly from the contemporary faith in economic enterprise as a force in itself promoting the common good. In 1882 Congress established a commission to negotiate with the Sioux for a division of the Great Reserve into tribal reservations and for a cession of remaining lands to the United States.[59] The report which the commission turned in on February 1, 1883, provided for a separation of the territory into five reservations, on which the Indians were to be settled with allotments larger than the treaty of 1868 stipulated; and for the cession of about eleven and a half million acres to the Government.[60] This agreement was so vigorously assailed by defenders of Indian rights both in and out of Congress that it was ultimately rejected by that body. The opposition was by no means hostile to the general purpose of the plan nor to the size of the cession. They denounced what they regarded as inadequate compensation to the Indians and a failure of the commission to live up to treaty requirements providing for a three-fourths vote of the Sioux adults for any revisions of existing agreements.[61]

As regards the general aim of the transactions, the Mohonk Conference in 1883 went on record in favor of a second and just agreement. The Conference recommended, ". . . that a cession of territory should be effected, by which a portion of the lands comprised within the limits of the Great Sioux Reserve might be thrown open to white settlement, and railroads be constructed to points west of the reservation. Such action, it was admitted, if wisely and justly carried out, would be beneficial not only to white men but to Indians."[62] Dr. Lyman Abbott told the Conference in 1885 that the reservations were obstacles to progress and that they should be reduced. He said, "The post-office is a Christianizing institution; the railroad, with all its corruptions, is a Christianizing power, and will do more to teach the people punctuality than schoolmaster or preacher can."[63]

In 1887 the agent at the Fort Peck office in Montana wrote, "The Montana division of the St. Paul, Minneapolis & Manitoba Railway, now being constructed east and west, through this reservation, will, in my opinion, have a greater tendency to civilize these Indians than any other one thing, for the reason that it will bring them in contact with the whites, the most of whom in this country are energetic, pushing people. They are amazed at the activity and endurance of the railroad workmen, and regard them as 'big medicine.' "[64]

The fifth annual report of the executive committee of

the Indian Rights Association in 1887 took note of both the triumph of allotment and the new railroad activity. The report is worth quoting at length on this subject:

> If any person accustomed to weigh evidence could still think it possible to maintain the old system of the isolation of the Indians, and to perpetuate the common ownership of their lands, a little reflection upon the relations of the railroads of the country to the Indian reservations would be sufficient to expel this delusion from his mind finally and forever . . . .
> This process of opening the reservations to railroads is certain to continue. In most cases the Indians themselves are in favor of it, thus showing that they have a truer conception of the meaning of civilization than is exhibited by the opponents of the severalty law. Most of the objections against this measure which have come to our notice show clearly that their authors are mere theorists, who have little knowledge of the actual condition of the Indians under the existing order of things. To maintain and perpetuate existing conditions is clearly impossible. It could not be done if we all united in an effort to that end. That was the reason for the enactment of the severalty law. We have to choose between securing something for the Indians—as much as we can get—or having them lose all. The friends of the new law think half a loaf better than no bread, even for Indians. But the law does not, as most of its enemies affirm, take the unallotted lands from the Indians. It leaves such lands in possession of the tribes, exactly as now.[65]

It is apparent from such statements that the friends of the Indian were well aware of the vital economic forces which were tearing down the old Indian system. It is impossible to say whether or not these philanthropists would have supported the allotment scheme if they had not been faced with the necessity of shaping some drastic new policy to protect the Indian against the expanding white settlement. The fact is that the theory of allotment fitted easily into the pattern of their idealism. It was at the same time a practical solution of the immediate problem. The friends of the Indian saw his only chance of surviving the economic conflict in his learning to cope with these forces of civilization on their own terms. And since civilization was good, this making of the Indian into a civilized man was also, in itself, good. The philanthropists knew it would be a case of "sink or swim" for the Indians. They accepted the fact, as they accepted the American civilization, that some of the Indians would go down. But these idealists believed that with some tutelage and support most of the Indians would emerge from the competitive struggle, purged and successful, as real Americans were supposed to do. So, from every point of view, the friends of the Indian saw allotment as his great American opportunity.

On the other hand, as has been shown, there is plenty of evidence to indicate that there were definite and powerful interests behind allotment which were not philanthropic at all; that homesteaders, land companies, and perhaps railroads, saw allotment as a legal way of getting at wide areas of Indian lands. To be sure the evidence is for the most part inferential. In matters of public policy, interests of this sort are never so articulate as are those supporting high causes. But there is the basic fact that white settlement and enterprise were irresistibly sweeping westward; and the fact that allotment was used to remove Indians from valuable lands. There is no evidence that any of these private interests originated the allotment idea. Had it been for them to choose, they would have probably preferred outright dispossession. But they were certainly not hostile to allotment or there would have been western opposition to it in congress; and the Dawes bill would not have progressed through its final stages almost without debate and passed without a roll call.

In conclusion, let it be said that allotment was first of all a method of destroying the reservation and opening up Indian lands; it was secondly a method of bringing security and civilization to the Indian. Philanthropists and land seekers alike agreed on the first purpose, while the philanthropists were alone in espousing the second. Considering the power of these land-seeking interests and their support by the friends of the Indian, one finds inescapable the conclusion that the allotment system was established as a humane and progressive method of making way for the "westward movement."

# CHAPTER III

## ORGANIZATIONS
## SUPPORTING ALLOTMENT

The Board of Indian Commissioners was established by act of Congress in 1869 to participate with the Indian Office in the expenditure of Indian funds and to exercise general powers of advice and supervision.[1] It was composed of public-spirited citizens, appointed by the President, who could be trusted to have the best interests of the Indians at heart and who should serve without pay. This organization served to focus public interest in Indian problems, and it generally supported allotment after its first expression of approval in 1876.[2]

The first strictly private and propagandist society of importance to be organized on behalf of the Indian was the Women's National Indian Association which came into existence in 1879.[3] Its twin aims as formulated in 1883 were to stir up public sentiment in favor of Indian rights and by educational and missionary work to hasten the "civilization, Christianization and enfranchisement" of the Indians themselves.[4] The national society was primarily a federation of local branches, the number of which was listed in 1886 as seventy-odd.[5] Predominantly eastern in its origin, the organization gradually extended its hold beyond the Alleghenies.

It depended heavily upon church support, especially the Protestant sects. In 1885 one of the Women's National Indian Association's prominent leaders said, "From the beginning the appeal was to Christians, to pastors of churches, and to editors."[6] Although in 1882 the society presented to Congress a petition with 100,000 signatures urging the strict observance of Indian treaties and from time to time reported other political activities, the women seem especially to have engaged in educational and missionary work.[7] By 1884 they were spending somewhat over $2,000 a year.[8] They worked in close cooperation with the Indian Rights Association and the Woman's Christian Temperance Union, with whom, in spirit and organization, they seem to have had much in common.[9] The Women's National Indian Association early espoused the cause of allotment. Indeed, in 1887 the president of the society quoted Senator Dawes as saying that the present Indian policy was "born of and nursed by" the Women's National Indian Association.[10] Their report in 1884 mentioned the fact that the Indian Rights Association had "fallen heir to the years of work previously done by the Women's National Indian Association."[11]

The Indian Rights Association was organized in December, 1882, at a meeting attended by thirty or forty men who had assembled to consider ways and means of educating the public and Congress in the business of promoting Indian welfare. This meeting decided on three objectives: More general education of the public, legal protection for the Indian, and a "wise division of land in severalty."[12] The Association emphasized its educational work, as the women did.

In 1886 the Indian Rights Association printed 50,000

pamphlets and conducted numerous meetings.[13] They apparently did not engage in missionary work in the field. They were preoccupied with shaping white attitudes and policies and therefore with legal and political action. They kept investigators at work, and they maintained a lobbyist in Washington.[14] The Association's report for 1886 states, "The Association seeks to arouse public sentiment in behalf of justice for the Indian through the dissemination of reliable information, and, when this sentiment is aroused, to concentrate its influence upon Washington."[15] To these ends the Indian Rights Association spent $8,700 in 1887.[16]

To the general student of this period the comparison is interesting between the relations of the Indian Rights Association and the Women's National Indian Association in the movement for Indian reform with the relations between the Anti-Saloon League and the Woman's Christian Temperance Union in the prohibition movement at a somewhat later date. In both cases the women's societies were on the ground first and continued to make their greatest contribution in the shaping of public attitudes. The men's groups, on the other hand, were most effective and valuable in practical political action. Very similar to the spirit of the Anti-Saloon League was the temper of the Indian Rights Association, which its secretary described in 1886: "The Indian Rights Association represents practical and business-like aims and methods for the solution of the Indian problem. It has no interest in extreme or eccentric theories or plans."[17]

It would be hard exactly to divide the credit between the Women's National Indian Association and the Indian Rights Association for the passage of the general allotment law. It seems clear that both these organizations contributed to the achievement. Although the women thought Senator

Dawes had awarded them the first palm, the Indian Rights Association declared in 1887, "In securing the passage of this law the Indian Rights Association achieved the greatest success in its history."[18] There seems to be no doubt but that the women had prepared the way and that the men had been most effective in their dealings with Congress. Professor C. C. Painter, the Indian Rights Association's Washington representative, had been busily on the job urging legislators to support allotment.[19] Apparently it was a combination of the activities of most of the Indian rights defenders that was responsible for the passage of the Dawes Act. Senator Dawes told the Lake Mohonk Conference in 1887, "It should be called the Mohonk Bill, that is the name of the bill; it is the inspiration of the people, you are responsible for it. . . ."[20]

The first Lake Mohonk Conference was summoned by the Honorable Albert K. Smiley, member of the Board of Indian Commissioners, who toward the end of 1883 invited to his lake resort men and women prominent in Indian reform movements. He explained his action to the Conference in 1885. He said, "My aim has been to unite the best minds interested in Indian affairs, so that all should act together and be in harmony, and so that the prominent persons connected with Indian affairs should act as one body and create a public sentiment in favor of the Indians."[21]

Annually to this meeting came members of the pro-Indian organizations, of religious bodies, and of philanthropic societies, and other public leaders. The first meeting, in 1883, declared at once for a general allotment law, and up through 1887 this project occupied much of the attention of the Conference.[22] There were from time to time disagreements as to detail, but the consensus of friends of the Indian heartily supported the general allotment scheme.

There seem, however, to have been protests from informed circles. In 1887 the Indian Rights Association referred to these objectors as "obstructionists."[23] Apparently some of them were anthropologists and ethnologists. At the fourth Lake Mohonk Conference, in 1886, one member said that opposition to allotment came in some measure from "the desire of the ethnological student to preserve these utensils for the study of his specialty." He went on to say, "Perhaps, in the face of Miss Fletcher's noble work among the Omahas, I may not do this (condemn all anthropologists). Certainly her philanthropy swallowed up her anthropology."[24] The writer has so far been unsuccessful in finding any express declaration against allotment by the anthropologists of the period. There was a society which was organized in 1885 under the name of the Indian Defence Association. This group was opposed to the immediate breaking up of reservations. The second resolution in their "platform" said, "That in the present condition of the mass of the Indians to confer upon him the title to his lands in severalty would not supply to him the motive and means of industry adequate to contend with the disadvantages of his condition and surroundings, while the motives to part with his land would be in the great majority of cases irresistible."[25]

However, the society proposed that lands be patented to tribes in trust "to secure permanent individual occupation and industrial use, and ultimately to enure, in severalty, to the Indians on a principle of distribution according to age and numbers."[26] Apparently this society was in agreement with other defenders of the Indian in their belief as to the ultimate solution of the Indian problem, but the organization regarded immediate allotment as too precipitant. The distinction was vital to the society and it explained its reason for organizing as follows: ". . . the fact that powerful organizations are already the advocates of the policy to be opposed renders it necessary that the effort to counteract their influences should be an organized effort also."[27] Among the officials of this ephemeral society was at least one professional ethnologist, the Reverend J. Owen Dorsey, who wrote many monographs on Indian social institutions, and who was a staff worker in the American Bureau of Ethnology.[28] It is interesting to note that another member of this organization's executive committee was John H. Oberly, then Superintendent of Indian Schools, who that same year made the above-quoted eulogy of individualism at the Mohonk Conference.[29]

All ethnologists were not, however, opposed to the allotment movement. Miss Alice C. Fletcher, who was referred to above as a philanthropist, spent more than thirty years studying and working among the Omahas. In collaboration with the son of an Omaha chief she wrote a fascinating account of that tribe, which was printed by the Bureau of American Ethnology.[30] She was known to have been the person primarily responsible for the Omaha allotment act of 1882.

In 1881, John Wesley Powell, Director of the Bureau of American Ethnology, expressed his approval of allotment in a letter to Senator Morgan, saying, "No measure could be devised more efficient for the ultimate civilization of the Indians of this country than one by which they could successfully and rapidly obtain lands in severalty . . . ."[31] So the Indian Rights Association, after castigating the "obstructionists" in 1887, was able to go on to say, ". . . the enlightened sentiment of the country is undoubtedly in favor of the law and its enforcement."[32] In other words, most everyone seems to have been enthusiastic about allotment—except the Indian.

# CHAPTER IV

## INDIAN ATTITUDES
## AND CAPACITIES

No one should expect, of course, an informed and eager opinion about allotment from the Indian. Alien as he was to the white man's way and ignorant of his aims, the Indian would hardly welcome at first glance the civilized substitutes for his economy, ideals, and culture. However, it was the policy of the Indian Administration to regard the Indians as anxious for the establishment of the allotment system. In 1881 the Commissioner, in a letter to Senator Nathaniel P. Hill, listed the particular tribes that had petitioned for allotment and concluded by saying, ". . . it may truthfully be said that there are at this time but few tribes of Indians, outside of the five civilized tribes in the Indian Territory, who are not ready for this movement."[1] As early as 1876 agents were reporting Indian sentiment in favor of allotment and presenting Indian petitions, and this activity increased up to 1887.[2] In 1880 the House Committee on Indian Affairs favorably reported a bill allotting lands in severalty to the Miamis and Peorias. The report said that the bill had been drawn and introduced at the instance of the Indians themselves and that all revisions of the bill had been made in conference with representatives sent by the two tribes to Washington.[3] In 1881 the Omahas presented their petition, signed by fifty-five men of the tribe.[4] The reports of the agents indicate that as the Indian came more in contact with white settlement and got some experience in individual holding he was often readily won over to a support of the allotment system. For instance, the Yakima agent in Washington Territory reported in 1886 that but a few years before a majority of the Indians were so hostile to allotment that they would pull up the surveyors' stakes "almost as fast as they were driven." But now nine-tenths of the Indians "would gladly welcome" allotment.[5]

From the repeated statements of those Indians who favored allotment it is clear that what was first and foremost in their minds was a hope that patents in fee would protect them against white inroads upon their lands and against the danger of removal by the Government. A comment as early as 1876 from the Siletz agent in Oregon as to his charges' desire for allotment is typical. He said: "Nothing gives them so much uneasiness as the constant efforts of some white men to have them removed to some other country."[6] There seems to have been little understanding of or desire for a new agricultural economy on the part of the Indians. This was quite as true of the Omahas, who at the time were regarded by white proponents of allotment as especially enlightened. One of the fifty-five members of the tribe who asked for allotment expressed his sense of the changing order by concluding his statement (as nearly all the fifty-five did) with the usual argument. He said: "The road our fathers walked is gone, the game is gone, the white people are all about us. There is no use in any Indian thinking of the old ways; he must now go to work as the white man does. We want titles to our lands that the land may be secure to our children."[7]

There were many expressions of Indian opposition to allotment in the early 1880's. The minority report of the House Committee on Indian Affairs in 1880 noted that since the act of 1862 provided for special protection of allottees in their holdings it was "surpassing strange" that so few had availed themselves of their privileges.[8] The Senecas and the Creeks made bold to memorialize Congress against disrupting with allotment their systems of common holding.[9] Realizing that they were opposing the trend of official policy, the Creeks remarked: "In opposing the change of Indian land titles from the tenure in common to the tenure in severalty your memorialists are aware that they differ from nearly every one of note holding office under the government in connection with Indian affairs, and with the great body of philanthropists whose desire to promote the welfare of the Indian cannot be questioned."[10] The Shawnees, whom their agent represented as a "self-supporting . . . honorable, industrious people," were very anxious to preserve their tribal economy in 1883.[11] Even the Omahas, of whom fifty-five members had urged allotment, were, according to Miss Fletcher, originally opposed to allotment by a majority of two-thirds. Her explanation sounds very real: "It means trouble at first, and Indians are, like the rest of mankind, unwilling to vote for present trouble in order to secure an unknown and uncertain benefit."[12]

Certain tribes had specific objections to allotment. A memorial from the Creeks, Choctaws, and Cherokees in 1881 read: "The change to individual title would throw the whole of our domain in a few years into the hands of a few persons."[13] Senator Dawes explained to the 1885 Mohonk

Conference that since a railroad charter foolishly provided for a strip of land twenty miles wide through Indian Territory in case the Indian title should become extinct, the Five Civilized Tribes were suspicious of the Government and disinclined to have any dealings with it in questions of land title.[14] The Iowas in 1881 were against any scheme to allot land to their half-breeds because of a previous sorry experience when this class had been given allotments, had rapidly squandered them, and had then returned to live off the tribe.[15] The Senecas frankly preferred their old way of tribal philanthropy. Their council in 1881 passed a resolution against allotment and in favor of retaining their communal system. The resolution said: "Under this [communal] system no Indian, however improvident and thriftless, can be deprived of a resort to the soil for his support and that of his family. There is always land for him to cultivate free of tax, rent or purchase price."[16]

It is difficult to analyze and weigh the motives of the Five Civilized Tribes in their particular opposition to allotment. Samuel Taylor, in his study of the Dawes Act, maintains that white cattlemen, who had secured special privileges from the sovereign nations of Indian Territory, were responsible for the latter's opposition and were indeed influential finally in getting the Five Tribes exempted from the provisions of the general allotment law.[17]

In those days the charge was often made that under the tribal system in Indian Territory certain Indians had cornered for their own use large tracts of land and being therefore powerful in their communities they had succeeded in persuading the tribal government to oppose allotment which would redistribute the land. The Commissioner of Indian Affairs wrote in 1886: "At present the rich Indians who cultivate tribal lands pay no rent to the poorer and more unfortunate of their race, although they are equal owners of the soil . . . . It will not do to say, as the wealthy and influential leaders of the nation contend, that their system of laws gives to every individual member of the tribe equal facilities to be independent and equal opportunity to possess himself of a homestead. Already the rich and choice lands are appropriated by those most enterprising and self seeking."[18]

On the other hand, that same year the agent to the Five Tribes explained the land system in his report, saying that while tracts were occupied by and inherited by individuals, such possession was dependent on use. He concluded:

> Although this tenure of lands may seem strange to those who have not seen its qualities tested, it is a proposition which, from a public standpoint, might well be argued as superior to the fee simple in the individual. This system precludes a possibility of unjust pauperism so often imposed on worthy labor by force of modern circumstances or ancient customs surviving in modern times. However this question may be argued by political economists, there is no doubt in my mind that this is the true safeguard for the Indian people until they have grown, under the educational influences now working, up to the capacity of full American citizenship, until they are able to cope with that most ingenious of all thieves, the insidious land swindler.[19]

The most usual argument of the Indians against allotment was that it interfered with their established tribal system. Senator Teller rather oratorically declared in 1881: "I say to-day that you cannot make any Indian on this continent, I do not care where he is, while he remains anything like an Indian in sentiment and feeling, take land in severalty."[20] This statement is partially substantiated by the

44

fact that opposition was likely to come from the full-bloods and older generations whereas allotment was more popular among the half-breeds and younger people.[21] Agents usually referred to the former group as "conservatives" and the latter as "progressives." Agents frequently commented on this division of opinion and several times attributed the defense of the old order to the machinations of chiefs and headmen who feared allotment would mean tribal disintegration and a consequent loss of their power. James G. Wright of the Rosebud Agency wrote in 1885: "The old 'fogies' or 'chiefs,' who look to their supremacy and control over the people, fearful of losing it, discourage and advise the people to continue in the old rut. It is a contest between the old stagers and the young and progressive, with the prospect of disregarding the 'chiefs,' and the young men assuming the responsibility of their own acts."[22]

The last statement may suggest some of the difficulties in the way of coming to a conclusion about a general Indian point of view concerning allotment. There was clearly no one point of view. Particular attitudes were shaped by particular situations, experiences, factional disputes, specific opportunities. There is above all the fundamental difficulty of determining what the sentiment of a tribe actually was. Petitions are no reliable index. The Omaha petition of 1881 for lands in severalty apparently was not representative of the tribe.[23] In 1882 Chairman Dawes of the Senate Indian Affairs Committee reported that the Umatillas had long desired allotment, that tribal chiefs had come to Washington in 1879 to ask for that privilege.[24] Yet in 1885 the Commissioner of Indian Affairs noted that in three different tribal councils called in that year by special agents and commissioners the Umatillas had rejected an allotment agreement. The regular Umatilla agent thought that this action was the result of the above-mentioned hostility of the mixed-bloods and of stockmen and others interested in the prevailing reservation set-up.[25] There is a final fact which must be taken into consideration in interpreting reports of Indian sentiments and of the results of allotment experiments, namely, that allotment had become an official policy. As Senator Teller maintained with probable accuracy, there would be a tendency on the part of agents and subordinate officials to be influenced in their estimates consciously or unconsciously by the knowledge that allotment was the program to be furthered.[26]

What can be said from this survey is that there was no apparent widespread demand from the Indians for allotment. It should not be surprising that the greater number of Indians should be adversely disposed or apathetic in regard to the new policy. There were groups that for particular purposes favored allotment. Many were undoubtedly influenced by the persuasion of agents and other officials who were supporting the new program. On the other hand, there were Indian vested interests opposed to the change. And there was the inertia of a whole tradition stretching backward for generations. One could hardly expect the mass of Indians to be able to comprehend and desire a complete new way of life which their white friends had envisaged for them.

What has been said above about the difficulties in evaluating the accounts of Indian attitudes applies even more drastically to the assaying of reports about the success and failure of allotment experiments up to 1887. There are numerous testimonies to the success of these ventures. The Commissioner's description of the White Earth Reservation in 1880 indicated that those Indians had approached what their white friends probably regarded as an ideal Indian community. At least some of these Indians cultivated their lands in severalty. The Commissioner wrote: "Nearly all at White Earth wear citizen's dress, live in houses, send their children to school, attend church on the Sabbath, and lead a quiet, industrious, agricultural life. Many have surrounded themselves with the comforts of civilized life, and a casual observer would notice but little difference between their settlement and the white farming communities of the frontier."[27]

The reports of many agents declared that their respective charges were, as a result of allotment, approaching this ideal, as the following samples will show.

The Devils Lake agent, Dakota, 1881: "Nearly all of them are located on individual claims, living in log cabins, some having shingle roofs and pine floors, cultivating farms in severalty, and none are now ashamed to labor in civilized pursuits. A majority of the heads of families have ox-teams, wagons, plows, harrows, &c., and a desire to accumulate property and excel each other is becoming more general."[28]

The S'kokomish agent, Washington Territory, 1881: "[The issuing of certificates] has gratified them very much and stimulated them to do more clearing than in former years. There has scarcely been an idle man on the reservation during the summer, and drunkenness among those living here is almost entirely unknown."[29]

The Mackinac agent, Michigan, 1885: "The Indians are beginning to realize the value of these lands, are more eager to get them, and retain them more tenaciously than heretofore. They are farming better, and keep a sharp lookout that the agent does not allot land to those not entitled, being anxious that it shall be saved for their children."[30]

The Crow Creek and Lower Brule agent, Dakota, 1886: "Allowing these Indians individual tracts of land has proved very beneficial, by giving them some idea of the rights of property, and causing them to take more pride in their homes and possession . . . . Young people are asking for claims so soon as they arrive at legal age."[31]

In 1880 the Commissioner observed that even some of the wildest Indians were taking to farming in severalty and to civilization. He wrote:

Except a few Indians who possessed houses and culti-vated fields in the vicinity of Fort Sill, the Kiowas, Co-manches, and Apaches have moved up to the Washita, and are settling down, not as before in large crowded camps, but in small groups and by families, and they are opening up separate farms instead of cultivating one large body of land in common. In this way tribal relations are being modified and the influence of chieftainship impaired . . . . A willingness to dispose of ponies for articles more helpful to civilization, and a disposition to adopt citizens' dress, are most favorable indications.[32]

There seem to have been many examples of Indians who were struggling to learn the white man's way. Most of the fifty-five Omahas who petitioned for allotment in 1881 made such statements over their signatures. On the whole these statements seem quite authentic. The following is worth quoting in part:

When I was a boy I saw much game and buffalo, and the animals my forefathers used to live upon, but now all are gone. Where I once saw the animals I now see houses, and white men cultivating the land; and I see that this is better. I ought long ago to have tried to work like the white man; but for several years I have been trying, and perhaps in the future I can do much better for myself and my friends. . . . I want a title for my land. I am troubled about it, for I am not sure I can have the

48

land if I do not get a title. . . . In the morning I get up
and look at my fields, and I wish that God may help me
to do better with my land and let it be my own.[33]

In this connection, the writer suggests that a valuable
study might be made of Indian attitudes toward and profi-
ciency under the allotment system in terms of their particular economic backgrounds. The attitudes and adaptability
of Indians as regards allotment might bear some ascer-
tainable relation to the fact of their having been nurtured
in primarily agricultural, pastoral, or hunting economies.

But alongside of accounts of Indian progress under allotment schemes there were conflicting reports and many dec-
larations that experiments had been utter failures. There
were even disputes as to the success of the allotment system
among the Omahas. Long before the Allotment Act of 1882
these Indians had under previous treaties begun to abandon
their villages and cultivate farms in severalty.[34] In 1884 the
Indian Administration began an experiment in partial self-
government among the Omahas to accompany the policy
of independent holdings.[35] In 1884 and 1885 there were
testimonies given by the agent and Miss Fletcher that the
Omahas were getting along well.[36]

However, the new agent sent to the reservation in 1886
took issue with these statements and reported that things
were going badly.[37] Apparently the Commissioner did not
agree with this latter view, for in his report of the same year
he said that on the whole the success of the Omahas was
such as "to afford to Indians everywhere the highest en-
couragement to adopt the same policy."[38] Apparently the
Omaha situation was a complicated one, involving factional squabbles and all sorts of adjustments under the new
political regime.[39] Very possibly the agent was expecting
too much.[40]

49

There were many unequivocal statements of the failure of allotment before 1887. In 1883 a Creek memorial to Congress quoted Secretary of War Lewis Cass as saying in 1835 that allotment experiments which permitted the alienation of lands had "wholly failed."[41] Indeed his generalization would have been equally true in 1887. Where Indians had the right of selling their lands it was in the nature of things that those lands should slip from their grasp. In 1878 the Mackinac agent said that a treaty of 1855 had granted lands in severalty to certain adult Chippewas but "through the shameful neglect of the agents then and since in charge, they have frittered a large proportion of them away, and to-day, I am of the opinion, not one in ten who have had these lands owns an acre, and they are as poor as if they had never owned them."[42] In his report of that year the Commissioner noted that five-sixths of the 1,735 Chippewas in Michigan who had received patents had lost their lands.[43]

A member of the Board of Indian Commissioners said in 1886 that titles in fee had been granted for nearly all the lands of the Isabella Reservation in Michigan and of the 86,200 acres so allotted only 2,000 acres were left in the Indians' hands.[44] The critical Senator Teller declared in 1881 that although over sixty treaties had provided for allotment in severalty since 1845 there were perhaps but three or four places where Indians had taken individual holdings and were still living on them.[45]

Of course, the advocates of allotment were well aware of this particular peril of the lands' being dissipated, but they confidently hoped to guard against it by restricting alienation for at least twenty-five years. However, there was evidence that legal restriction had not been effective in protecting Indian lands. The minority report of the House Committee in 1880 pointed to the example of the Catawbas whose land titles had been restricted from alienation for twenty-five years. The report said, "The Catawbas gradually withered away under the policy, until there is not one of them left to attest the fact that they ever existed, and their lands fell a prey to the whites who surrounded them and steadily encroached upon them."[46] In 1881 a petition from the Five Civilized Tribes cited the case of the Shawnees, Potawatomis, and Kickapoos living in Kansas who had been allotted lands with the proviso that they could not be sold for twenty years unless the Indians became citizens. The petition stated that in five years every acre had been sold to white men and the tribes had to be shipped into Indian Territory.[47]

But according to various accounts the alienation of lands was but one of the failures of allotment. In 1883 the Creek memorial to Congress quoted figures purporting to show that Indian population declined more rapidly under the allotment system. The figures showed that in certain instances an augmented decrease in population was coincident with the period of allotment and that in some cases an actual gain in population occurred after allotment had been discontinued.[48] But such figures are very unsatisfactory. Too many factors enter into the question of births and deaths to allow any certain correlation with allotment experiments in this period. Indeed there are no statistics before 1887 that are of use in attacking the problem.

The greater number of testimonies to the failure of the allotment system suggest that the fundamental obstacle to the policy's success lay in the Indians' attitudes toward civilized economy. The Indian simply did not take easily to the idea of becoming a citizen and an independent farmer. In 1876 the agent at the Great Nemaha Reservation said the Sac and Fox Indians were refusing to take allotments because they did not want to assume the obligations of citizenship.[49] Agents found it difficult to get the Indians to keep their minds on their work. The Fort Berthold agent wrote in 1885: "They seem to tire quickly, and are constantly offering excuses to be absent from their work, either to look for a lost pony or to visit some sick relative, or some other frivolous excuse. It is on this account that they require constant attention, and it is only by a constant drive, which we have given them, that they have accomplished so much."[50]

The Fort Peck agent in 1885 found his Indian farmers lacking in the proper patience and restraint. He wrote: "The most of them have a great desire to eat their corn and potatoes and other vegetables before they get ripe, and many of them go in the night time and get their own vegetables, and then say that some one else has taken them. To prevent this I have stationed the police as much as possible at the proper places to protect the crops."[51]

The Indians of the Sisseton Agency in Dakota first took up their allotments of course with no real sense as to the use and value of the land. The agent explained how in 1876 the Indians in making their choices selected tracts which seemed to promise the easiest supply of fuel, water, and shelter. So they huddled together in ravines and along the wooded shores of lakes. Many of their allotments did not contain the fifty acres of arable land which had to be under cultivation before an allottee could receive a patent. In 1884 the agent was trying to persuade them to move out onto the fertile prairie.[52] Such testimony as this suggests very vividly what easy prey the Indians were to the land sharks.

The Commissioner in 1886 was aware of the cultural and temperamental obstacles to the progress of Indian independent farming. He wrote: "A majority of the grown-up Indians on reservations, through want of early training and by reason of repugnance to any kind of manual labor, which their traditions and customs lead them to look upon as degrading, are very poor material out of which to make farmers." He made the following important addendum: "It must be understood, also, that many of them are located on reservations where the soil is poor, or no regular rains fall, or the climate is so severe and the seasons so short that it would be a difficult matter for a first-class white farmer to make a living."[53] Thus it is no wonder that confronted with the requirement that they toil and in the sweat of their brow eat their bread the Indians should often feel a nostalgia for the old life and all its ways. An agent in 1879 noted that the Otoes and Missourias were trailing behind other tribes in agricultural progress. He wrote: "They seem unwilling to give up the hope that they may yet return to the free and unrestricted life of their forefathers, and fear the development of farms and improvements will prevent the realization of that hope."[54]

The ideology of that departed life had included no real concept of property in land. To almost all Indians the land was "Mother Earth," and attaching to her property concepts would indeed have seemed sacrilegious.[55] Furthermore, in their basic pastoral and hunting economy there was no need or room for the civilized idea of landed property. There are Indian legends that reveal a remote agricultural past, and when the white man first came to America he found the Indian growing maize and vegetables all through the temperate regions from the Atlantic to the Rockies.[56] But with the exception of the Pueblos the Indians of modern times derived their livings primarily from herding and the chase. Gardening was a drudgery for the squaw and not

53

a dignified work for a warrior and huntsman. Where agriculture had been developed, the idea of the less deified "soil" took form, but theories of ownership never seem to have gone beyond a vague recognition of a right to an area, based on use and occupancy.[57]

One can therefore imagine the difficulties which the supporters of allotment encountered in implanting in the Indian mind that proprietary sense which was fundamental in the white economy. The agent to the Poncas, Pawnees, Otoes, and Oaklands, in Indian Territory, wrote in 1886: "As a whole, however, the Poncas recognize no especial claim to their allotments, holding only that the land is the tribe's, in common. This matter of allotments to them of their lands in severalty is quite a favorite and hackneyed theory, and may be an exceptionally good one, but the practical features connected with it are not unattended by difficulties of considerable moment."[58] The minority report of the House Committee in 1880 expressed more definite convictions about the matter. It read:

> From the time of the discovery of America, and for centuries probably before that, the North American Indian has been a communist. Not in the offensive sense of modern communism, but in the sense of holding property in common . . . . The very idea of property in the soil was unknown to the Indian mind . . . .
>
> This communistic idea has grown into their very being, and is an integral part of the Indian character. From our point of view this is all wrong; but it is folly to think of uprooting it . . . through the agency of a mere act of Congress, or by the establishment of a theoretical policy.[59]

The authors of the report were avowedly concerned more with matters of practice than of theory, but however they might define "communism," it seems clear that the Indians had been perhaps more communal in their general living than they had been in property notions. The Yankton agent in Dakota in 1887 found the traditional Indian neighborliness very disturbing so far as agricultural progress was concerned. "They want to be together," he said. He told of seeing eight Indian teams in a less than eight-acre lot cultivating—between convivial rounds of sitting and smoking. He noted that all eight teams accomplished less in a day than one white man could. He had seen forty neighbors gathered around a threshing machine on which not more than ten men could work at a time. At the noon meal all were on hand, and at the end of the day everyone expected a sack or two of meal for lending his "gracious presence to the occasion." Under this system the owner of the field reaped for himself but a small fraction of what he had sown. The agent noted another annoying cultural survival. "The grass dance," he said was still going on. These were occasions for the debauching of young girls and furthermore for the giving away of valuable property, "which is utterly at variance with the civilizing influences of successful farming." These "festivities of their pagan life" would continue, he thought, until these Indians were settled on their allotments. And he concluded, "That cohesion, which is bred of idleness, of a common history, a common purpose, and a common interest, and unites the Indians in a common destiny, must be broken up before dancing will cease."[60]

In conclusion, it can be said that the allotment policy had not been generally successful before 1887. It is understandable that optimistic observers with faith in allotment as an ultimate solution of the Indian problem should have been cheered by any small gains that they saw. No one could have expected of course an immediate and wholesale success after so revolutionary a change. Furthermore, the friends of the Indian had espoused the theory in the first place without great deference to the facts of experience. Their hopeful visions always projected the Indian as he should become, to the exclusion of seeing what he had been. To deny this assertion is to imply that the friends of the Indian were weak or insincere in their support of allotment, that they had knowingly advanced the interests of those who would despoil him of his lands. For allotment had not worked well from the first. In 1879 the Commissioner had reported to Secretary Schurz that in cases where Indians had been granted patents—even restricted patents—"with very few exceptions" the allottees had "fallen victim to the cupidity of the whites" and had been defrauded of their lands. Characteristically, however, he observed that allotment in itself had many times been successful as a civilizing agent.[61] The conflicting sentiments in these assertions reveal the whole psychology of the friends of the Indian. They looked at failures in the allotment system as they, and other philanthropists, looked at failures in the American competitive society—with genuine regret but with the unshaken conviction that individual enterprise was the God-given way of civilization. For the friends of the Indian, the act of 1887 was an act of faith.

CHAPTER V

THE APPROACH
TO THE NEW POLICY

The passage of the Dawes Act was of course the occasion for rejoicing and high expectations on the part of the friends of the Indian. In September, 1887, the fifth Mohonk Conference resolved: "The passage of the Dawes bill closes the 'century of dishonor.' "[1] President Cleveland in his annual message the following year said: "No measure of general effect has ever been entered on from which more may be fairly hoped, if it shall be discreetly administered."[2] There was no doubt in the minds of the proponents of the allotment system that they were on the road to the complete solution of the Indian problem. When Professor Painter at the fifth Mohonk Conference suggested a complete reorganization of the Indian Service by putting absolute control in the hands of a board of commissioners, Senator Dawes went so far as to say that the general allotment law had obviated the need for tinkering with the organization of the service. He said: "It seems to me this is a self-acting machine that we have set going, and if we only run it on the track it will work itself all out, and all these difficulties that have troubled my friend will pass away like snow in the spring time, and we will never know when they go; we will only know they are gone."[3]

Indeed this "self-acting machine" would finally render obsolete all government machinery whatever. Senator Dawes went on to express a prediction of which an echo has been heard in discussions of the present proposed policy:

> Suppose these Indians become citizens of the United States with this 160 acres of land to their sole use, what becomes of the Indian Reservations, what becomes of the Indian Bureau, what becomes of all this machinery, what becomes of the six commissioners appointed for life? Their occupation is gone; they have all vanished, the work for which they have been created . . . is all gone, while you are making them citizens . . . . That is why I don't trouble myself at all about how to change it [the machinery of administration].[4]

Dr. Lyman Abbott said: "The Indian is no longer to be cared for by the executive department of the government; he is coming under the general protection under which we all live, namely, the protection of the courts."[5]

But while Senator Dawes was sure that their new machine was traveling in the right direction, he did not expect it to run itself. At this same Mohonk Conference he said: "Don't say, we have made this law and it will execute itself. It won't execute itself." He went on to plead for educating the Indian to his new way of life.[6] In other words, the solution of the Indian problem was to involve the withdrawal of government control accompanied by an active policy of helping the Indian to meet his new opportunities and the problems of his new freedom. Furthermore, the supporters of allotment were pretty much alive to the importance of proceeding cautiously and slowly in the application of the policy. The opponents of the original Coke bill had assailed it as a doctrinaire measure which sought to apply an untried theory wholesale and indiscriminately to all Indians. The minority report of the House Indian Affairs Committee said in 1880 that the Coke bill would erect "a Procrustean bed" which all Indians would be cut to fit.[7] But in 1887 those who had worked for the general allotment law were soberly considering the responsibilities which their victory had brought them.

Senator Dawes had said to the Mohonk Conference in 1885, "When you have set the Indian upon his feet, instead of telling him to 'Root, hog, or die,' you take him by the hand and show him how to earn his daily bread."[8] The Indian Rights Association said of the Dawes bill in 1886, ". . . we deem it necessary to call public attention to the fact that the mere enactment of such a law is only the enlargement of opportunity. It does not, in itself, change the condition of a single Indian."[9] In 1887 the Board of Indian Commissioners reported:

> The law is only the seed, whose germination and growth will be a slow process, and we must wait patiently for its mature fruit. There are difficulties and perplexing questions to be settled and conflicting interests to be adjusted. Some of these are found in the character and habits of the Indians themselves, while many are ready and have been waiting long for this beneficent measure; some non-progressive Indians are still opposed to it, and will throw obstacles in the way of its execution. They see their power and importance as tribal chiefs slipping away, and they have enough human nature to cling tenaciously to their prerogatives.[10]

The Commissioner expressed similar sentiments in 1887 and concluded by noting that the President had wisely ordered that allotment be applied only where Indians were known to be favorable to it.[11] But, alas, as Senator Dawes pointed out, the pressure was too strong for even the President to proceed at a measured pace. Instead of applying allotment to but one reservation, he had applied it to half a dozen by the end of September.[12] By the end of the year twenty-seven reservations had been selected to work out the new system.[13]

The friends of the Indian, then, realized in 1887 that their job had hardly more than begun. Senator Dawes told the fifth Mohonk Conference that it was responsible for the passage of the allotment law, "and the Mohonk Conference," he said, "is responsible to-day for what shall take place in consequence of it." There was considerable talk of the need for further laws to give the Indian special legal protection in his new state. Senator Dawes thought that the allotment act was all the legislation necessary and if the Government would but "act with" the new system, all would go well.[14]

Nevertheless, the Conference finally resolved that further legislation was required to guard the Indian in his rights and "to prevent his new liberty and opportunity from becoming a curse instead of a blessing."[15] President Edward H. Magill of Swarthmore believed that the religious organizations must bear the brunt of preparing the Indian for civilized life. As for Government he said, "All that we can ask of it, at present, is not to be a hindrance, while it cannot become a help."[16] The Reverend Charles Shelton quoted President Cleveland as saying, "No matter what I may do; no matter what you may do; no matter what Congress may do; no matter what may be done for the education of the Indian, after all, the solution of the Indian question rests in the Gospel of Christ."[17] Yet Bishop Frederic D. Huntington of New York had already told the Conference, "I have not known, these eighteen or twenty years of my acquaintance on the reservation, of a single instance of a real devout Christian character . . . . Not a man or woman have I found who makes spiritual life uppermost and foremost, and who are tender and strong in their attachment to Christ."[18]

Almost all of the supporters of allotment agreed that the great need of the Indian was to be education—of some sort. Some of the more realistic of the Indian's friends saw the importance of immediate and practical farm training. Senator Dawes had said in 1885: "It is now supposed that you can take an Indian against his will—by the nape of his neck, if I may say so—tell him to be a farmer and then go off and leave him, but you can't make anything of him under that process. An Indian will not make much of a farmer unless he can be inspired with a desire to be one, and unless you show him how. It is a work of time . . . ."[19]

At the 1887 Mohonk Conference Miss Fletcher and Professor Painter both showed themselves aware of the Indian's need for industrial education.[20] Indeed the general subject of education was the dominating theme at that conference. But to most of the speakers it seemed that education meant chiefly Christianizing, the teaching of English, and training in morals and citizenship. For instance, the anti-climax of Dr. F. F. Ellinwood's following remarks is striking:

> Now I take it that, having the Dawes' Bill as a law, the process of disintegration will go on by causes and influences with which we need not concern ourselves. I take it that the greed of the Anglo-Saxon, and of the white man generally, is so strong that these reservations will be disintegrated just as fast as it is possible to overcome all restrictions . . . . But, sir, the moral and religious

aspect of this question is the one with which we are concerned here to-night.[21]

Five of the eight resolutions adopted by the Conference dealt with education, and especially religious education, the burden of which was to be carried by church organizations.[22]

The Commissioner was very much aware of the new role education was to play in the administration of Indian affairs. In his report for 1887 he said: "The progress made in school work during the year has been most gratifying, and the interest in education, both among Indians and their friends, has clearly received a new impetus from the passage of the law providing for lands in severalty and citizenship."[23] The Commissioner went further to state the aims of Indian education:

> There is not an Indian pupil whose tuition and maintenance is paid by the United States Government who is permitted to study any other language than our own vernacular—the language of the greatest, most powerful, and enterprising nationalities beneath the sun. The English language as taught in America is good enough for all her people of all her races ....
>
> The adults are expected to assume the role of citizens, and of course the rising generation will be expected and required more nearly to fill the measure of citizenship, and the main purpose of educating them is to enable them to read, write, and speak the English language and to transact business with the English-speaking people .... True Americans all feel that the Constitution, laws, and institutions of the United States, in their adaptation to the wants and requirements of man, are superior to those of any other country; and they should understand that by the spread of the English language will these laws and institutions be more firmly established and widely disseminated.[24]

In general it is fair to say that the friends of the Indian in their first enthusiasm for fitting him to live in the new system established by the Dawes Act laid emphasis first on his being a citizen and second on his being an agricultural worker. This, again, was part of the whole prevailing socio-political theory. America was the land of the free. The Government should guarantee civil equality and then every man would have his opportunity to forge his own way to success.

# CHAPTER VI

## THE DEVELOPMENT
## OF AN EDUCATIONAL POLICY

It is worthwhile to give some time to a consideration of the policy of Indian education as it was worked out through this period. The whole allotment project was an educational project. Its success or failure depended upon the success or failure of its educational policy. Although this truth was never lost sight of by the genuine friends of the Indian, the great degree of failure which their allotment scheme encountered was caused chiefly by the fact that their educational system failed in two vital respects. In the first place, education could not keep up with allotment. As has appeared above, the pressure brought to bear on the Government by interested whites prevented the intelligent planning and leisurely pace which should have characterized the execution of the allotment program. In the second place, the educational ideas of the friends of the Indian, although expressive of the highest motives, were but slightly related to the essential needs of a primitive people confronted with civilization. The whole educational theory supporting allotment was premised by the belief that in all respects the Indian should be treated as a white man. Moreover, the fundamental ideas of American education—for white or Indians—which dominated this period of history are being quite generally questioned by the present generation. Tragically enough, the education of the Indian which was planned for his liberation not only failed to reach its aim but contributed to his further subjection. It was an education adapted to a dominant race—or class—to the strong, aggressive, and able.

The year 1888 was marked by a greatly increasing interest in Indian education on the part of philanthropic groups. The Board of Indian Commissioners urged the importance of the subject, and the Mohonk Conference spent most of its three days in a consideration of it. There was much talk about establishing one unified system of Government education, instead of the hodge-podge of Government schools, mission schools, and contract schools.[1] But the only proposal that the Commissioner made in his report that year was the admirable one of dividing the boarding school dormitories up into smaller units, where the girls would learn housekeeping and the boys, gardening. However, the Commissioner struck the keynote of the official policy which was to be developed. He said:

> The Indian child must be taught many things which come to the white child, because of environment, without the school-master's aid. From the day of its birth the child of civilized parents is constantly in contact with civilized modes of life—of action, thought, speech, dress —and is surrounded by a thousand beneficent influences that never operate upon the child of savage parentage, who, in his birth-hour, is encompassed by a degrading atmosphere of superstition and of barbarism. Out from the conditions of his birth he must be led in his early years into the environments of civilized domestic life. And he must be thus led by the school teacher.[2]

The Mohonk Conferences during the ensuing years furnished a forum for the threshing out of educational theories. The extreme individualism and laissez faire was represented in the ideas of Captain Richard H. Pratt, who, interestingly enough, was superintendent of Carlisle. In 1881 he had expressed himself in favor of immediate and compulsory allotment because he believed that the Indian would make no progress until he got his land, squandered it, and had to buckle down to hard work.[3] From time to time he repeated this theory in one form or another. In 1891 he said to the Conference, "I would blow the reservations to pieces. I would not give the Indian an acre of land. When he strikes bottom, he will get up. I never owned an acre of land, and I never expect to own one."[4]

But this was certainly an extreme view, which few others seem to have shared. Yet it shaded off into the educational theory which placed emphasis upon "character" rather than upon industrial training. President Merrill E. Gates of Amherst College said to an 1892 conference of Indian sympathizers, over which he was presiding, "Such workers as Miss Fletcher and Capt. Pratt come to us and say, 'Make more of the manhood of the Indian and think less of his property.' . . . I think the fact that he and Miss Fletcher and others lay the emphasis on man's personality and the kind of training that comes through trying to walk alone, through tripping and falling, through learning how easily property may be lost, should be carefully considered."[5] Miss Fletcher regarded allotment as an educational enterprise itself. She told the Conference in 1890, "But allotment itself is an education; it startles an Indian and makes him feel that it is time for him to stir himself . . . . I do not feel afraid of severalty."[6] General Samuel C. Armstrong, superintendent of Hampton, agreed with her. He said, "There is a philosophy in that severalty business that people do not understand or realize. We teach citizenship as we teach swimming. An ounce of experience is worth a pound of theory."[7]

It was a favorite theory of the friends of the Indian that education would come to him through allotment especially because of his coming in contact with white settlement. Speaking of the allotment law, President Cleveland said in his annual message of 1888, "Contact with the ways of industrious and successful farmers will, perhaps, add a healthy emulation which will both instruct and stimulate."[8] These sentiments were often expressed. Indeed, plans were again and again proposed for speeding up and multiplying these contacts. When the Reverend J. M. Buckley, D. D., editor of the *Christian Advocate*, remarked, "It must, of course, take ages to transform the Indians into beings resembling us," Captain Pratt said, "How long would it take to assimilate them if we went about it with all our forces? Not more than from three to five years. We have plenty of room. It would only make nine Indians to a county throughout the United States."[9]

In 1890 ex-Justice William Strong of the United States Supreme Court said to the Board of Indian Commissioners' conference, "I would, if I had my way in the matter, plant no allotment of an Indian family within 10 miles of another."[10] The more experienced humanitarian, Miss Fletcher, rose to attack this drastic proposal. She said, "We can not take an Indian up by the scruff of his neck and put him where we please. He has his home, such as it is, and his associations, and they have to be respected. There is a great deal in the Indian's life and efforts that one must be careful not to destroy, for it will not do to destroy too much when trying to reconstruct a people."[11] She proceeded to say that it was her policy to group relatives as much as possible on allotments. General John Eaton at the 1889 Mohonk Conference expressed for those times an exceptional point of view. He said:

> Let me allude to another fact which should be brought out in this connection,—the lack of attention on the part of all our Indian movements as to the Indian family. Now, I want to know, from those of you who have been most intimate with the Indian, In how many cases can you find the history of the family? In how many cases can you, when getting the land in severalty, state the relation of those who are to inherit that land from the first patent? I believe, among the persons who have been at work for some time in carrying on this work of location in severalty, only one—Miss Alice Fletcher—has comprehended this idea, and begun to make a record of the children, and the relation of the uncles, aunts, and cousins to the parties benefited. It seems to me that there needs to be an emphatic movement on the part of this Conference, seconding this proposition of universal education reaching the family of the Indian, that that fundamental agency appointed by the Almighty may be properly used in the great transformation which we seek.[12]

A program of assimilation, called the "outing system," was developed at Carlisle. It was a scheme of sending Indian children out to live in white homes. Captain Pratt often sang the praises of this system. On one occasion he said that the system should be extended until every Indian child was in a white home, and presto! the whole Indian problem would be solved.[13] Miss Fletcher thought that the outing system had contributed to the success of allotment. She said in 1890: "It is easier to convince the young men who have had attrition with the east. It is one of the advantages of the outing system that it shows the Indian what a civilized community means in the development of a country."[14] She found the returned student invaluable when it came to persuading the older Indians to accept allotments.[15]

The friends of the Indian, following the good pedagogical tradition, pinned their faith on the rising generation. In 1894 Professor Painter explained that the clause providing inalienability for twenty-five years had been put in the Dawes Act to assure the land's remaining in Indian hands "until the old men should have passed away, and the sons and daughters shall be educated to appreciate the value of it, and then dispose of it if they wish, but not sooner."[16] For the most part, then, the allotment proponents hoped that the mere ownership of the land would educate the adult Indian to its use, but in any event the training of the young would lay the foundations for the future realization of all the blessings of the allotment policy.

There were some, however, who felt the need for an active policy of adult Indian education, especially for practical agricultural training. Particularly did this feeling find expression when some of the first results of the allotment policy began to appear. President Gates said to the 1890 Mohonk Conference, "The only education we gave the Indian by our laws regarding *land*, was to give him a training in the process of being systematically robbed."[17] Two men who were skeptical about the exclusive concentration on the education of the young—who sensed the futility of trying to educate the youth to carry on a system which was disintegrating around them while they were being educated —were Senator Dawes and William H. Lyon, chairman of the purchasing committee of the Board of Indian Commissioners. In 1890 Mr. Lyon appealed to the Mohonk Conference in behalf of adult Indian education and the

following year he said to the meeting, "The great importance of educating Indian children, and the different
methods suggested, have been fully discussed; but very little
has been said, except by Senator Dawes, about educating
the adult Indians in a way by which they can become self-
supporting. I think education for the adult Indians in agricultural pursuits is very important, and, in my judgment,
it has been greatly neglected."[18] At an 1890 conference of
the Board of Indian Commissioners Senator Dawes again
expressed his fears that the allotment of lands was going
forward too precipitately, before certain Indians were prepared for it. He quoted a Commissioner of Indian Affairs
as saying that "he never supposed it was incumbent on him
to see that every Indian was fitted to take care of himself."[19]
Senator Dawes that same year challenged the Mohonk
Conference:

What have you done to prepare these people for their
new home and for their new state? Hardly anything can
any of you call to mind,—anything that the Government,
that the friend of the Indian, that anybody, has done to
prepare an allottee for life on his allotment. The only
persons that I have met who fully comprehend the necessity of preparing a new home before the old one falls
down are those women who, under the inspiration of
Miss Fletcher and Mrs. Kinney, have accomplished so
much in building houses for the Indian. What has been
done outside of that has been little more than to set the
wild Indian out on one hundred and sixty acres of land
and leave him there. What is he to do? He has no cover-
ing over his head, no horse, no plough, no hoe, no seed.
He never held a plough in his life, and still you put him
there and bid him farm. No: the one thing which presses
upon my mind more than any other, and has been from
the beginning, the one thing I have suffered criticism for

in many places, not excepting my own home, is the necessity of preparing the allottee for the allotment. I sometimes think you had better abandon the allotment altogether and keep him where he is, unless this is done.[20]

In 1889 General Thomas J. Morgan was made Commissioner of Indian Affairs, to the great joy of the friends of the Indian. He received the enthusiastic endorsement and continued support of the Mohonk Conference and of religious organizations.[21] The cattlemen and "boomers" of Indian Territory were said to regard the new Commissioner as an "Eastern crank,"[22] and the Senate withheld approval of his appointment until he had promised to be cautious in his educational reforms.[23] Commissioner Morgan had a special interest in education. In 1891 he wrote in his report "When I assumed charge of this office I held the opinion that the solution of the Indian problem lay chiefly in the line of education and that consequently one of the most important functions of the Commissioner of Indian Affairs was the perfecting of the scheme for bringing all Indian youth of suitable age under proper instruction. Accordingly I have given to this subject my most earnest attention during the more than two years of my administration."[24] The Commissioner's interest was not primarily in adult vocational training but in educating the Indian youth along American lines—in citizenship and "culture." In December, 1889, he presented to the Secretary of the Interior a special report on education. Since his ideas were generally approved by the friends of the Indian and since therefore his ideas reflect the point of view directing the working out of the allotment policy, it seems worthwhile to quote several excerpts from this report. The following items are culled from his statement of aims and purposes:

When we speak of the education of the Indians, we mean that comprehensive system of training and instruction which will convert them into American citizens, put within their reach the blessings which the rest of us enjoy, and enable them to compete successfully with the white man on his own ground and with his own methods. Education is to be the medium through which the rising generation of Indians are to be brought into fraternal and harmonious relationship with their white fellow-citizens, and with them enjoy the sweets of refined homes, the delight of social intercourse, the emoluments of commerce and trade, the advantages of travel, together with the pleasures that come from literature, science, and philosophy, and the solace and stimulus afforded by a true religion . . . .

The Indian youth should be instructed in their rights, privileges, and duties as American citizens; should be taught to love the American flag; should be imbued with a genuine patriotism, and made to feel that the United States, and not some paltry reservation, is their home . . . .

Education should seek the disintegration of the tribes, and not their segregation. They should be educated, not as Indians, but as Americans . . . .

Co-education of the sexes is the surest and perhaps only way in which the Indian women can be lifted out of that position of servility and degradation which most of them now occupy, on to a plane where their husbands and the men generally will treat them with the same gallantry and respect which is accorded to their more favored white sisters.[25]

As to policies and methods of education, Commissioner Morgan advocated nothing radically new. He gave expression to what were generally prevailing theories about the Indians. But he did give impetus to the extension of the Indian educational system. His ideal was to establish a standardized school system in which attendance would be universal and compulsory and which in other respects as well would be a replica of the American public-school system. He wrote, "So far as possible there should be a uniform course of study, similar methods of instruction, the same textbooks, and a carefully organized and well-understood system of industrial training . . . . The system should be conformed, as far as practicable, to the common-school system now universally advocated in all the States." All Indians looked alike to him. First and foremost, they were alike in this one important respect: they were all in need of being made over into the image of the white American. And Commissioner Morgan was hopeful. He said, "It is no longer doubtful that, under a wise system of education, carefully administered, the condition of this whole people can be radically improved in a single generation."[26]

In his recommendations concerning the various grades of Indian schools, Commissioner Morgan carried his theories to their logical conclusions. He did not neglect the importance of vocational training. He said that the high schools should teach the domestic arts, agriculture, and machinery for "without machinery the Indians will be hopeless and helpless in the industrial competition of modern life." The grammar schools should acquaint the girls with household duties and the boys with farming and the trades. The report went on to say, "Labor should cease to be repulsive, and come to be regarded as honorable and attractive. The homely virtue of economy should be emphasized. Pupils should be taught to make the most of everything, and to save whatever can be of use. Waste is wicked."[27] The Commissioner's recommendations and the tone of his remarks indicate that vocational training, as the rest of education, was to be a matter of teaching the Indian the white man's way—of teaching him to take his place in the economy of civilization. There is no mention of Indian arts and crafts.

But in harmony with the prevailing outlook of the friends of the Indian and with American educational theories in general, the Commissioner was really concerned with moral, civic, and "cultural" education. He wrote: "While, for the present, special stress should be laid upon that kind of industrial training which will fit the Indians to earn an honest living in the various occupations which may be open to them, ample provisions should also be made for that general literary culture which the experience of the white race has shown to be the very essence of education." With reference to Indian high schools he said, "The chief thing in all education is the development of character, the formation of manhood and womanhood. To this end the whole course of training should be fairly saturated with moral ideas, fear of God, and respect for the rights of others; love of truth and fidelity to duty; personal purity, philanthropy, and patriotism." He said further, "The Indian needs, especially, that liberalizing influence of the high school which breaks the shackles of his tribal provincialism, brings him into sympathetic relationship with all that is good in society and in history, and awakens aspirations after a full participation in the best fruits of modern civilization. The high school should lift the Indian students onto so high a plane of thought and aspiration as to render the life of the camp intolerable to them. If they return to the reservations, it should be to carve out for themselves a home, and to lead their friends and neighbors to a better mode of living. Their training should be so thorough and their characters so formed that they will not be dragged down by the heathenish life of the camp."[28]

Americanization in the Indian grammar school was to be pushed to what seem today to be grotesque extremes. A few excerpts from the Commissioner's report will suffice:

School-rooms should be supplied with pictures of civilized life, so that all their associations will be agreeable and attractive. The games and sports should be such as white children engage in, and the pupils should be rendered familiar with the songs and music that make our home life so dear. It is during this period particularly that it will be possible to inculcate in the minds of the pupils of both sexes that mutual respect that lies at the base of a happy home life, and of social purity. Much can be done to fix the current of their thoughts in right channels by having them memorize choice maxims and literary gems, in which inspiring thoughts and noble sentiments are embodied.

It is of prime importance that a fervent patriotism should be awakened in their minds. The stars and stripes should be a familiar object in every Indian school, national hymns should be sung, and patriotic selections be read and recited . . . . They should be made familiar with the lives of great and good men and women in American history, and be taught to feel a pride in all their great achievements. They should hear little or nothing of the "wrongs of the Indians," and of the injustice of the white race. If their unhappy history is alluded to it should be to contrast it with the better future that is within their grasp . . . .

Everything should be done to arouse the feeling that they are Americans having common rights and privileges with their fellows. It is more profitable to instruct them as to their duties and obligations, than as to their wrongs . . . .

No pains should be spared to teach them that their future must depend chiefly upon their own exertions, character, and endeavors . . . . Society will recognize in them whatever is good and true, and they have no right to ask for more. If they persist in remaining savages the world will treat them as such, and justly so . . . .

The school itself should be an illustration of the superiority of the Christian civilization.[29]

The friends of the Indian interested themselves after 1889 particularly in the extension of the Indian-school system. In its report of January 31, 1889, the Board of Indian Commissioners urged compulsory education for all reservation Indians.[30] In October the Commissioner of Indian Affairs read to the Mohonk Conference the special report which he subsequently submitted to the Secretary of the Interior.[31] The report was enthusiastically received, and the following year the Commissioner was able to set down a long list of important educational leaders and organizations that had approved his program.[32]

In 1892 Congress passed a law permitting the Commissioner to enforce rules and regulations of attendance at Indian schools and the following year provided that the Secretary of the Interior might withhold rations or other annuities from Indian families that failed to send children to school.[33] These measures had the warm endorsement of the Mohonk Conference.[34] In 1889 the Commissioner wrote concerning the cost of Indian education, "The Government of the United States, now one of the richest on the face of the earth, with an overflowing Treasury, has at its command unlimited means, and can undertake and complete this work without feeling it to be in any degree a burden."[35] It was a worthy appeal to the famous "Billion Dollar Congress," and the following year the legislators responded by raising the appropriation for Indian education thirty-five percent and thereafter, except for the lean years following the panic, gradually increased the sum until the Government was spending $3,000,000 for the purpose at the beginning of the twentieth century.[36]

But there was no such expenditure of money and effort in the vocational training of adult Indians—in spite of Senator Dawes and Mr. Lyon. During a discussion of the legal status of the Indian and the future heirship problem, Senator Dawes said to the 1890 conference of the Board of Indian Commissioners, "I would concentrate the thought of the philanthropic and energetic friends of the Indian upon the single idea. How fast and by what means can you fit individual Indians for the opportunity which the law holds open to them to become self-supporting citizens of the United States? I would let the other questions go."[37] That year he told the Mohonk Conference that the proceeds from the sale of surplus Indian lands should be used to buy agricultural supplies and to pay additional farming instructors, instead of being distributed among the members of the tribes.[38] In 1891 Commissioner Morgan emphasized the importance of preparing the Indian for his allotment and said, "Land in severalty without education may prove a bane rather than a blessing."[39]

But what he seems really to have meant by education was that sort of training in morals, citizenship, and the arts which is sketched above. In 1889 the Commissioner noted with satisfaction that Congress had appropriated money for additional farmers to instruct the Indians, and that year he sent out a letter of inquiry to each agent, asking about the work of his farmers.[40] But the Commissioner put forward no comprehensive plan for agricultural education among the Indians, nor did anyone else. The only attempt which the Government made along these lines was from time to time to make appropriations for "additional farmers" on the reservations. The white "farmer" and the "stock-man" had been long since established as regular agency and school employees.[41] In 1884 Congress appropriated $25,000 for the pay of "practical farmers" in addition to the regular agency farmers at a salary not exceeding seventy-five dollars a month to "superintend and direct farming among such Indians as are making effort for self-support." Two years later this amount was raised to $40,000. It was further raised in 1888 to $50,000, in 1890 to $60,000, and in 1891 to $70,000. In 1896 the appropriation was cut to $65,000 but the maximum salary was also reduced to sixty-five dollars a month.[42] Congress provided this amount annually thereafter into the twentieth century.

It is apparent that the appropriation for the agricultural instructors, whether it was $65,000 or $70,000, was pitifully inadequate for an effective carrying out of vocational training. In 1890 the Rosebud agent reported that he had two additional farmers but needed six to do the work properly. He wrote that such an increase in his staff would bring to each family the visit of a farmer once a week instead of once every two or three weeks. Other agents made similar requests.[43]

Mr. Lyon said to the 1891 Mohonk Conference, "There are good teachers for the schools, but very few to teach farming. The Indian needs to be taught how to use a plough and a shovel and an axe. He can not get a living off the land without this instruction. The only solution of that difficulty is to get farmers for instructors."[44]

In 1897 the Board of Indian Commissioners urged Congress to provide for increasing the number of farmers to teach the 60,000 Indians that had been allotted land, but their plea produced no effect.[45] There were 241 employees in the Indian Service listed as "farmers," in 1887, 272 in

1897, and 320 in 1900.[46] In other words, at the opening of the century there were 320 farming instructors to minister to the wants of 185,790 Indians, exclusive of the 84,754 members of the Five Civilized Tribes to whom the Government was not yet furnishing this service.[47] And it had been the official theory that most of these Indians were to become agriculturists. In 1900 there were 343,351 acres of land actually cultivated by Indians.[48] The consequences of this lack of proper instruction are suggested in the comments of the Rosebud agent in 1890. He wrote, "Unless Indians are so located that the farmer can be amongst them all the time but little can or will be accomplished, as during his absence, which may be for two or three weeks, an Indian breaking an implement becomes discouraged and awaits his return."[49]

Nor was it true that the farmers made up in quality for what they lacked in quantity. Through this period the system of political appointments produced a crop of farmers who were concerned more with politics than with agriculture.[50] In 1890 the Commissioner recognized that the farmers were not all that they might have been, and he thought that they might have accomplished more if they had been selected with more care and had been given better facilities and supervision.[51] Miss Fletcher remarked in 1892 that the farmers' work "would stand improvement."[52] Agents referred in their reports very seldom to the quality of the farmers' service.

But there were occasional complaints. In 1895 the Tulalip agent spoke of the "incompetency and carelessness" of his farmers, and the superintendent of the Seneca boarding school in Indian Territory claimed that the position of farmer at the school had invariably been occupied by men whose capacities were no greater than those of a "tinker or chore boy."[53] In 1914 the Commissioner felt it necessary to send a circular letter to reservation superintendents informing them that farmers were to be employed in practical instruction in agriculture and not in clerical positions. The Commissioner remarked, "It is almost discouraging to contemplate that after years of employment of men who have been especially charged with the work of advancing the farming interests of the Indians not more has been accomplished."[54]

In conclusion, it may truly be said that whatever the intrinsic merits or flaws of the allotment system the Government failed utterly at the crucial point of the program's administration. The Government and the friends of the Indian, realizing generally the need for education in the allotment program, failed to provide the Indian with that basic vocational training by means of which, only, could he have become a self-supporting farmer. The proponents of allotment thought that if they could catch the Indian young enough, train him in a school in white culture and American citizenship, he would as a matter of course turn out an independent, ambitious farmer. As for the old people, the mere possession of land could be trusted to work the miracle of turning a nomad into a husbandman.[55] Of course the result was generally failure. While the young were being educated, their parents' farms disintegrated. The graduates left the schools with educations that had shattered their traditions and substituted little that was real, and they returned home in quest of the "main chance" to find a demoralized community. These young Indians were faced with a dilemma which was more hopeless than that confronting the American youth, who so often returns with an education to a society which does not really value that education. It was not with an old entrenched order that the Indian youth had to contend. It was with social disintegration. It is not to be wondered that most of the young Indians succumbed.

There are two main reasons for the Government's shortsightedness in its Indian educational policies. In the first place, those who had been most articulate in the shaping of the Indian program—the idealists—were dominated by a point of view which had limitations that few of them could surpass. Their well-meaning tenet of individualism, which within the white society itself was not fostering the greatest good for the greatest number, was certainly not the solution of the Indian problem. But these people believed that if the Indian could be made to acquire all that American culture which was founded in individualism and competition, his salvation would be assured. In the second place, there had been powerful forces at work to destroy the reservation. Land-seeking settlers and wealthy business enterprises probably favored the allotment system as a means of freeing Indian lands. They were not primarily concerned with promoting Indian welfare. Once allotment was established, they would not be expected to spend much thought and time, and certainly not much money, in the improvement of the Indian so that he might be better equipped to stand up against them in business competition. They would agree with Commissioner Morgan that the right kind of education for the Indian was the implanting of Americanism. There were a few realists among the friends of the Indian, but for the most part he had no one to show him how he might really, in the end, come into his birthright.

# CHAPTER VII

## THE APPLICATION
## OF ALLOTMENT

The application of allotment to the reservations was above all characterized by extreme haste.

In September 1887—seven months after the passage of the Dawes Act—the author of the measure told the Lake Mohonk Conference how President Cleveland had remarked when signing the bill that he intended to apply it to one reservation at first and then gradually to others. Senator Dawes went on to say: "But you see he has been led to apply it to half a dozen. The bill provides for capitalizing the remainder of the land for the benefit of the Indian, but the greed of the land-grabber is such as to press the application of this bill to the utmost . . . . There is no danger but this will come most rapidly,—too rapidly, I think,—the greed and hunger and thirst of the white man for the Indian's land is almost equal to his 'hunger and thirst for righteousness.' "[1]

There were various reasons for this haste. For one thing, it is clear from Senator Dawes's remarks that the pressure of the western land-seekers and business promoters was steady and powerful, forcing the Government to a faster pace in the business of opening up Indian lands. Nor did the Government seem to move reluctantly; nor were restraining hands stretched out. In the first place, there was the feverish hurry which a political administration feels when it has a program to carry out. Senator Dawes said to the 1890 Mohonk Conference:

Within the last six years there have been four different Commissioners of Indian Affairs, each one having his own policy and his own convictions of the best methods of administering those affairs, and bound to carry out those convictions. I knew one Administration that in four years changed the policy of the Indian Bureau three times. The Administration is, therefore, bound to adopt that policy which it can complete within four years, if possible, or at least so far advance in that as to secure its completion, and not trust to the chances of the future or to the policy that successors may take up and carry out.[2]

In the second place, it must be remembered that most of the leaders in the allotment movement fundamentally believed that legislation had solved their problem. The general allotment law meant that the Indian was assured an opportunity to make his way in the world, which was all that an American asked. What reason would there be for delay in starting the Indian on the free high road to wealth and civilization? This prevailing faith in the almost automatic efficacy of allotment made it possible for the Government to yield in this instance to irresistible pressures with a clear conscience. The same economic and social forces which Carl Schurz had shown in 1881 to be pushing the Government into adopting the allotment policy were now hastening its application.[3] Very suggestive are the comments of Commissioner Morgan in his report of 1891. The Commissioner, who was known as a reformer and an "eastern crank," wrote concerning the need for reducing the reservations:

> Whatever right and title the Indians have in them [their lands] is subject to and must yield to the demands of civilization. They should be protected in the permanent possession of all this land necessary for their own support, and whatever is taken from them should be paid for at its full market value. But it cannot be expected under any circumstances that these reservations can remain intact, hindering the progress of civilization, requiring an army to protect them from the encroachments of home-seekers, and maintaining a perpetual abode of savagery and animalism. The Indians themselves are not slow to appreciate the force of the logic of events, and are becoming more and more ready to listen to propositions for the reduction of the reservations and the extinguishment of their title to such portions of the land as are not required for their own use.[4]

The point of view expressed in this statement would hardly encourage caution and delay in administering allotment. Indeed, for the general purposes of civilizing the Indian and of giving the white man land, the general allotment law was too slow.

In 1890 the Commissioner reported: "In numerous instances, where clearly desirable, Congress has by special legislation authorized negotiations with the Indians for portions of their reservations without waiting for the slower process of the general allotment act."[5] In 1888 Congress had ratified five agreements with different tribes providing for allotment and for the sale of surplus lands.[6] The following year Congress passed eight such laws.[7] A member of the Board of Indian Commissioners in 1891 estimated that the 104,314,349 acres of Indian reservations in 1889 had been reduced by 12,000,000 acres in 1890 and by 8,000,000 acres in the first nine months of 1891.[8] This rapid reduction of the reservations met with the approval of the friends of the Indian. In 1889 General Eliphalet Whittlesey, secretary of the Board of Indian Commissioners, informed the Mohonk Conference of the agreements which Congress had ratified and were about to act upon and which would release for sale millions of acres of Indian lands. He seemed generally pleased with this progress and apparently regretted that the Cherokees had not come to their senses and agreed to the sale of some 6,000,000 acres in the Cherokee Strip. He said, "There is a strong opposition on the part of the Cherokees; and that opposition will not be overcome for a year or two."[9] In official eyes this whole policy was completely justified. Commissioner Morgan wrote in 1890:

> This might seem like a somewhat rapid reduction of the landed estate of the Indians, but when it is considered that for the most part the land relinquished was not being used for any purpose whatever, that scarcely any of it was in cultivation, that the Indians did not need it and would not be likely to need it at any future time, and that they were, as is believed, reasonably well paid for it, the matter assumes quite a different aspect. The sooner the tribal relations are broken up and the reservation system done away with the better it will be for all concerned. If there were no other reason for this change, the fact that individual ownership of property is the universal custom among the civilized people of this country would be a sufficient reason for urging the handful of Indians to adopt it.[10]

The economics of these land transactions especially appealed to the Commissioner. His estimate of the area of reservations in 1889 was 116,000,000 acres. On these lands lived 250,483 Indians. He figured that 30,000,000 acres would give each Indian a 160-acre lot. Excluding the lands of the Five Civilized Tribes, the Government could sell the remaining Indian lands at $1 an acre and realize $66,000,000. The interest on this sum alone, at five percent, would pay the entire cost of Indian education, and the principal could be gradually applied to help the Indian develop his allotment.[11]

In the meantime, the work of applying allotment was pushed rapidly forward. In 1888 the Commissioner complained that allotment was being slowed up for want of sufficient appropriations, but he had nothing really to worry about.[12] His successor, Commissioner Morgan, was not one to allow allotment to drag. In 1888 the Commissioner had reported that 3,349 allotments had been approved since the passage of the Dawes Act.[13] There were 1,958 allotments approved in 1890, 2,830 in 1891, 8,704 in 1892; and in this last year Commissioner Morgan reported that since February 1887 the Indian Office had given its approval to 21,274 allotments.[14] In this same year, 1892, he told the Mohonk Conference that the allotments which were about to be made would bring the grand total of all the allotments which the Government had made to over 80,000. He concluded it was time to slow down.[15] His successors seem to have acted upon his advice until the opening of the new century, as the following figures show:

ALLOTMENTS APPROVED 1893–1900[16]

| YEAR | NUMBER | YEAR | NUMBER |
|---|---|---|---|
| 1893 | 4,561 | 1897 | 3,229 |
| 1894 | 3,061 | 1898 | 2,015 |
| 1895 | 4,851 | 1899 | 1,011 |
| 1896 | 4,414 | 1900 | 8,752 |

In the years prior to 1887 the Government had approved 7,463 allotments with a total acreage of 584,423; from 1887 through 1900 it approved a total of 53,168 with an acreage of nearly 5,000,000.[17] Commissioner Morgan's boast of 80,000 allotments had not materialized, yet it seems as if allotment had gone ahead fast enough. Certainly Indian lands were disappearing fast enough. In 1891 and 1892 the Commissioner's reports contained interesting samples of what allotment meant in terms of reducing the total amount of Indian lands. The following tables of acreage show the disposition of land on reservations as a result of special agreements:[18]

| | 1891 | | 1892 | | |
|---|---|---|---|---|---|
| | Potawa-tomi | Iowa | Sac and Fox | Cheyenne and Arapahoe | Sisseton and Wahpeton |
| Allotted | 286,494 | 8,658 | 87,683 | 529,682 | 310,711 |
| Open for settlement | 266,241 | 207,174 | 365,900 | 3,500,562 | 573,872 |
| Reserved for school funds | 22,650 | 12,271 | 25,194 | 231,828 | 32,840 |
| Reserved for other tribal purposes | 490 | 20 | 800 | 32,343 | 1,347 |

These figures suggest the rate at which Indian lands were being transferred to white ownership. Of the 155,632,312 acres of Indian lands in 1881, there were 104,314,349 acres left in 1890 and 77,865,373 in 1900.[19] Of course with the speeding up of allotment tribal lands were dwindling at an even faster pace. In 1900 5,409,530 of the total 77,865,373 acres of Indian lands were lands allotted in severalty. So satisfactory was the speed of allotment to the Board of Indian Commissioners that in 1891 it was contemplating a very early disappearance of Government supervision over the Indian. The Board's report stated in that year:

Another suggestion we venture to offer in connection with land in severalty, and that is the gradual closing up of Indian agencies. When patents have been issued and homesteads secured, when Indians are declared and acknowledged citizens, and are actually self-supporting, the supervision of the Government and the arbitrary rule of the agent may be safely withdrawn . . . . We make this suggestion, not as immediately practicable on a large scale, but as a working hypothesis, an ideal to be reached in the not distant future. In some cases it may be practicable very soon.[20]

This faith that the allotment system would mean an early decline of Government supervision and placing the Indian on his own responsibility continued to be expressed by the friends of the Indian through the 1890's. But the hope was not realized. In 1900 there were in existence sixty-one agencies—three more than in 1890.[21] But while the maintenance of the agency system was in large measure dependent upon the needs of the service, it was apparently even more dependent on the needs of the agents. The Indian Rights Association reported in 1900 that Commissioner William A. Jones had recommended to Congress the discontinuing of fifteen agencies but that the agents had been able to bring such pressure through their friends at the Capitol that Congress had agreed to the eliminating of only one.[22]

As regards the acceptance by the Indians of the universal allotment program, anyone who scans the reports of the agents is struck by the enthusiastic approval which they record. Beginning with 1887, the year of the Dawes Act, and running through the 1890's, agents again and again write that the Indians are delighted with the prospect of getting allotment and impatient for the work to begin.[23] The Board of Indian Commissioners reported hopefully in 1890: "All

Indians are not yet ready to take allotments or sufficiently advanced to make good use of homesteads if granted to them. But we believe that a majority now desire to enjoy the benefits of the act, and others will, within a few years, be prepared for its application, when they see its stimulating effect upon profitable industry and its influence in promoting better habits of life."[24]

There is no doubt that the idea of allotment was making headway with the Indians, but there is considerable doubt that its progress was the result of a spontaneous and widespread interest of the Indians in becoming hard-working American farmers. For one thing, there are indications that the ambitious agents were turning on the pressure. Agents quite naturally comment to that effect. For instance, the Klamath agent wrote in 1888 that 800 Indians had signed up for allotments when the advantages of the system were "pointed out to them."[25] In that same year the Yankton agent wrote about a determined opposition to allotment which was led by the old chiefs and which was successfully overcome by two companies of soldiers from Fort Randall. The agent concluded by remarking that when the survey was finished there was not one Indian on the reservation who did not want his allotment.[26] The Quapaw agent in 1887 reported, "We have talked 'allotment' on all suitable occasions, and, as a rule, the Indians are gradually coming to see that it will benefit both themselves and their children."[27]

This persuasion in its milder forms seems a natural procedure, nor would it be disquieting to an impartial critic if he believed it had a real educational value; if he believed it was a method of making the Indians want to be and know how to be, industrious farmers. But there is evidence which suggests that the high-pressure campaigns which were carried on by officials were aimed primarily at achieving "results." A member of the Board of Indian Commissioners who visited the Devils Lake Agency in 1891 wrote:

Brought up from time immemorial to regard any kind of labor with aversion, as the Sioux Indians on this reservation have been, it will necessarily require years of training to make them successful agriculturists, or even to eke out a living from the soil; but while this is so, they can in the interval not only sustain life, but acquire property by engaging in grazing. Soon after my arrival I met Judge Joseph R. Gray, special allotting agent for this reservation, who has succeeded in allotting nearly 63,000 acres of land without so much as a murmur from the allottee.[28]

And apparently the high-pressure campaigns were achieving results. The Osage agent wrote in 1892: "For the past two years a persistent effort has been made to induce them to locate a claim for each member of the tribe, establish the corners and issue to the claimant a certificate for the same. While the full bloods more especially have never consented that this should be done, yet the agitation has caused a general rush for the claims, until it is difficult to find one that has not been located."[29]

Where the Indians were not merely stampeded but more independently and purposefully desired allotment, their motives varied. There were probably many who saw individual landed property as an opportunity to become independent, prosperous farmers. But allotment, the white man's system, also appealed to many as a means of acquiring social prestige. The secretary of the Board of Indian Commissioners said to the Mohonk Conference in 1890, "The Indians are very proud of the papers they have already received from the government . . . . They regard themselves as owners of lands and as on an equality with their white neighbors. They feel they have taken a place they never occupied before."[30] And at that same Conference Senator Dawes revealed an Indian motive for seeking allotment which was fraught with dire forebodings for the future. He said:

> The Indian of to-day is not the Indian who was in this country when the present policy was inaugurated . . . . The Indian as an Indian has already disappeared in this country. He has partaken of the spirit of change. He begins himself to be uneasy. He is discontented; he is determined he will no longer stay in the places and ways of the Indian of ten years ago. He has caught the idea of selling his land. He has caught it of the white man. It has been found that the easiest way to negotiate with the Indians for a portion of their reservation is to propose to pay a part, if not all, of the purchase-money by distribution per capita among the Indians . . . . It might as well have been thrown into the Pacific Ocean, for any permanent good it would bring the Indian . . . .
>
> Twenty-five years ago the Indians could not understand the idea of allotment. Now they are crazy to have allotment, because along with it comes the provision that they may sell to the government the balance of their land.[31]

On the other hand, as before 1887, there were many Indians reported to be vigorously opposed to allotment. A sampling of agents' reports shows many recorded instances of Indian opposition continuing on into the twentieth century.[32] The motives of these dissident Indians were very much of the same variety as those of the obstructionists who were active before the Dawes Act was passed.[33] In 1887 the Commissioner concluded that Indian opposition would be prompted by four attitudes: Indians were loathe "to give up their savage customs"; they were suspicious of "any innovation upon their nomadic way of life"; they were ignorant of allotment's purposes; and their minds had been poisoned and their fears aroused by designing white men. The Commissioner noted that "a personal and selfish motive" had been found at the bottom of every case of Indian opposition which had come to the notice of the Indian Office.[34] The Commissioner fails to explain exactly what he meant by this last generalization, but it could hardly apply to the whole sweep of Indian opposition. It would seem that the Indian Office had not investigated intelligently a very representative selection of cases—if one can trust the information which emerges from the agents' reports. In these reports one senses, usually in spite of the agent, the Indians' instinctive fear of this white man's system. For instance, there was the frequently expressed fear that allotment would in one way or another end in the Indians' losing their lands. The Kickapoos, Potawatomis, and Absentee Shawnees still feared that under allotment their people would go the way of their profligate relatives who received allotments and ran through them quickly back in the 1860's.[35] In 1889 the secretary of the Wisconsin Indian Association told the Mohonk Conference how her organization had beaten a congressional measure which provided for a special allotment to the Oneida Indians. She said the ardent support of the bill by the constituents of a certain Wisconsin Congressman had made her organization suspicious. She went on to say:

> I visited the Oneidas on the Fourth of July this year. . . . The best educated among the Oneidas are afraid of allotment. The "fringers" of the reservation, the outside element, were in favor of it, had been in favor of the

Hudd Bill; but the conservative element were afraid that their lands might, even with allotment, be lost through additional legislation. Their great fear was that in the coming winter, or even later, some new legislation might allow the sale of their allotted lands, and they expressed great anxiety for the weaker Indians, and even for themselves, lest they might not be able to stand against the machinations of the whites, who were so interested in the five years' clause.[36]

There is considerable testimony to the fact that the Indians knew pretty well what the white man's system had meant for their race. One of the members of the Board of Indian Commissioners reported in 1890:

> The Osages as a tribe are almost unanimously opposed to taking their land in severalty. Eighteen years ago they purchased this reservation of the Cherokees for a home, and as such they want it to be. They argue that the time for such action has not yet come; that they are not prepared in any way to have white settlers for neighbors, and especially that variety of white men with whom it has been their misfortune to come in contact. About 250,000 acres of an area of over 1,500,000 is tillable land, the other is only suitable for grazing, and this they contend is no more than is needed for themselves and children.[37]

This refrain is repeated in the reports of various agents. The Indians were opposed to allotment because they feared white economic penetration (in the matter of both individual lands and tribal holdings) and they feared white cultural penetration. A majority of the Flatheads were fighting allotment in 1887 because they believed the Government would sell their surplus lands to whites, "thus breaking up their reservations and mixing the Indians up promiscuously with the white settlers."[38] The Coeur d'

Alene agent in 1887 expatiated upon the integrity and orderliness of the Indians in his charge and then remarked that their tribal council had voted unanimously against allotment, "saying they had always been friendly to the whites and wanted to remain that way but as yet they were not willing nor capable of mixing with them."[39] Indeed the most frequently mentioned source of Indian hostility to allotment was to be found in their sense of tribal solidarity and in their disinclination to give up their Indian ways.

The agent at Cheyenne River wrote in 1887 that a majority of his Indians were against allotment and that those who lived in the large camps were particularly opposed. He wrote, "A very few have been induced to leave the camps and take separate places, but, as stated last year, the Indians in these camps spend most of their time in dancing."[40] In that year the International Council of Indian Territory, to which nineteen tribes sent fifty-seven representatives, voted unanimously against allotment and the granting of railroad rights-of-way through their lands. The council's resolution on the allotment question, which was sent to the President of the United States, cited these tribes' "sad experience" with allotment and assailed the policy as one which would "ingulf all of the nations and tribes of the Territory in one common catastrophe, to the enrichment of land monopolists."[41] The Commissioner's report of that year attributed this opposition to the Five Civilized Tribes, who he said were exempted from the Dawes Act anyway and among whom were persons with large tracts of land which they would lose under an allotment system.[42] The year before, the agent to the Five Civilized Tribes had risen to the defense of their economic system, but his successor in 1892 corroborated the Commissioner's opinion and noted that

94

members of the Five Tribes were beginning to see that their tribal economy served the interests only of the few. He believed there was a growing sentiment in favor of allotment.[43] Nevertheless, there is a compelling ring to the appeal of the International Council of 1887:

> Like other people, the Indian needs at least the germ of political identity, some governmental organization of his own, however crude, to which his pride and manhood may cling and claim allegiance, in order to make true progress in the affairs of life. This peculiarity in the Indian character is elsewhere called patriotism, and the wise and patient fashioning and guidance of which alone will successfully solve the question of civilization. Preclude him from this and he has little else to live for. The law to which objection is urged does this by enabling any member of a tribe to become a member of some other body politic by electing and taking to himself a quantity of land which at the present time is the common property of all.[44]

The following year the agent to the Five Tribes observed that the half-breeds were becoming favorably inclined toward allotment, but, he said, "The full-bloods are against it, as a rule, as they fear it will destroy their present government, to which they appear attached."[45] This same cleavage which characterized Indian opinion before the passage of the Dawes Act is apparent all through the nineties.[46] This cleavage expresses the fundamental fact that the allotment controversy was a struggle between two cultures. With the irresistible penetration of the white civilization, the conflict within the tribes crystallized into two factions, the half-breeds and the full-bloods, the young and the old, the "progressives" and the "conservatives," the sheep and the goats.

The progressives seemed to be winning the day. A member of the Board of Indian Commissioners was confident of this in 1891. He wrote, "The taking of their land in severalty is a subject in which these Indians [at Fort Peck] do not seem to have much interest. Doubtless, if the scheme was fully explained and the benefits clearly set forth, there would be no objections on the part of the Indians so intelligent as these appear to be. Of course, it is a question of only a short time when assent to the proposition will be universal."[47] This prophecy proved to be right. But of course, the final appearance of this universal "assent" did not mean that the progressives had won the argument. It was the Government that won the argument. The agent to the Kiowas, Comanches, and Wichitas wrote in 1888, "These Indians seem to be without a single exception opposed to the allotment of their lands in severalty at present. I believe most of them realize, however, that the time is coming when they will have to yield to it."[48] Indians were able to see the time coming because of situations like the one which the Ponca agent reported in 1892. He wrote: "It is but justice to say much opposition was in the air, the Indians obstinately refusing to receive their allotments; but through persevering efforts 300 allotments have been made . . . ."[49]

The Yankton agent, who persuaded the Indians to take allotments by importing two companies of soldiers from Fort Randall, explained his technique of administration in 1888. He wrote: "Conciliation is always the best policy in dealing with Indians, but when this fails, with the Indians clearly in the wrong, prompt, decisive action becomes necessary. There must be no yielding to Indian whims nor compromise to gratify Indian caprice, at the sacrifice of law and good government."[50] There was however one instance when the Government acted decisively and when it was the Government and not the Indian that was clearly in the wrong.

In 1907 the Senate Committee on Indian Affairs conducted extensive hearings on the condition of the Mexican Kickapoo Indians. At the hearings copious testimony was presented to show that in 1891 the Government's representatives had forced upon the Mexican Kickapoos an allotment agreement to which they were violently opposed. It was shown that the Indian signatures to the agreement were for the most part forged and that there were numerous names included that belonged to no living Indians.[51] Perhaps entirely ignorant of all this, Congress had ratified the agreement.[52] But there was at least one agent who showed distrust of high-pressure tactics. The Ponca, Pawnee, Otoe and Oakland agent wrote in 1889: "I find from four years of experience, not lightly taken, that to substitute the ways of the white man for the ways of the Indian can not be achieved short of prolonged, very painstaking, and very patient work. Small faith in the advice or counsel of the white man remains with the Indian character to-day."[53]

# CHAPTER VIII

## ADMINISTRATION AND CHANGES
## IN POLICY: LEASING

Officials of the Indian Service saw much that was hopeful in the first results of the general allotment policy. The reports of agents pretty generally asserted that allotment was going well and the Indians were making long strides in farming. A typical statement is that of the Tulalip agent in 1889. He said that his Indians were taking "as much pride in their stock and crops as white farmers."[1]

Much emphasis was placed on the civilizing influence of allotment. The agent for the Crow Creek and Lower Brule Reservations seemed impressed with his Indians' progress on the white man's road. In 1888 he wrote:

The advantage of placing Indians on individual allotments can not be overestimated. Once gaining a proprietary right in a piece of land, the owner is immediately elevated above the common level, feels his importance, and takes to himself a commendable degree of pride. The "tipe mitawa" becomes "the home, sweet home," and a longing is stirred within the Indian breast for more of the sweets of civilization.[2]

The friends of the Indian were particularly enheartened

by the unexpected progress of the Crows. In 1890 Miss Fletcher told a Board of Indian Commissioners' conference that she thought allotment was by then in an experimental stage only among the Crows and she was not sure it could still be called an experiment there.[3] This was indeed a triumph, for in 1887 Senator Dawes had expressed to the Mohonk Conference his great surprise that the Crows had been one of the first tribes to be chosen for allotment, since he regarded them as "wretched" and "degraded." General Armstrong, of Hampton Institute, immediately corroborated this estimate and called the Crows "low down, darkminded, and savage."[4] Yet, at this 1890 conference the General took his cue from Miss Fletcher and quoted a hardheaded, realistic old Indian fighter as having been astounded at the way the Crows were progressing under allotment. General Armstrong believed this meant that three-quarters of the Indians were ready for allotment.[5] In 1889 the secretary of the Board of Indian Commissioners told the Mohonk Conference how well certain wild tribes were getting on under allotment and concluded that the Dawes Act was not a failure.[6] Commissioner Morgan judiciously commented in 1891: "I have seen nothing during the year to lead me to change my views as to its [allotment's] ultimate success, although doubtless the change will come with too great suddenness to some of the tribes."[7]

There were, however, critics among the friends of the Indian who felt that the Dawes Act still left much to be desired. Professor Painter read to the 1889 Mohonk Conference a paper entitled "The Indian and His Property," which assailed the legal and administrative restraints imposed upon the economic freedom of the Indian. Professor Painter wound up by saying: "His condition under the severalty law is no better than under the old reservation

99

system, unless it go so far as to destroy utterly the old conditions imposed by that system. A step is taken, it is true, in the right direction, but not long enough to take him out of his difficulties."[8] The president of the Westchester County Historical Society, of New York State, was so moved by the professor's arguments that he remarked: "We have fondly supposed that the passage of the allotment bill would be a panacea for almost every ill in this Indian problem; and, lo! Professor Painter tells us, and a little examination for ourselves will show us, that the last state of this man is likely to be worse than the first."[9]

Those who were dissatisfied with the results achieved by the Dawes Act saw various causes of failure. For one thing, the whole emphasis of the allotment policy was laid upon farming, and critics from time to time pointed out that large sections of the Indians' lands were not suitable for agriculture. In 1891 Miss Fletcher estimated that two-thirds of the Indians lived on lands of this sort.[10] The Reverend Thomas Riggs, of the Dakota Mission, said to the 1890 Mohonk Conference: "We have tried to turn hunters into farmers. We have tried this not only in a good country where it would be difficult enough to teach agriculture to an Indian, but on the plains, in regions where out of five years we may possibly have a good crop one year."[11] For another thing, the Government was continuing a policy which was a cause, as well as an index, of allotment's failure. A speaker at the 1890 Mohonk Conference described at length the evil consequences of the rationing system. He showed how it had pauperized the Indians and now deterred them from farming, since they feared if they raised crops the Government would cut down their allowances.[12]

The chairman of the purchasing committee of the Board of Indian Commissioners also addressed the meeting on the subject. He said that he had expected the allotment system would bring an annual decrease in the requisitions of meat and flour for the Indians. As a matter of fact, the requisitions had each year increased. He told how the Government, to encourage stockraising at the Fort Berthold Reservation, had built an enormous barn—a barn large enough to house cattle "from a thousand hills." Yet at that moment the Government was sending much larger rations of beef to that reservation than it sent before the barn was built. The speaker thought the barn was probably used for ponies. He said the whole trouble was a lack of good teachers.[13]

Many friends of the Indian who believed that the allotment system was not accomplishing all that it should were inclined to hold the Government responsible because of its failure to give adequate aid to the allottees. These critics charged that the Government put Indians on their allotments and expected them to farm without training, tools, or equipment. Professor Painter told the 1889 Mohonk Conference how one Indian, with several hundred acres which composed the grants to himself and family, found "that he had indeed a vast but unusable possession: a large land estate, but without teams, implements, money, houses, or experience, and consequently without power to utilize a foot of it."[14] It was not true that the Government made no efforts whatever to equip the Indians for farming. But it made very slight efforts. The appropriation act passed in 1888 provided for the allocation of $30,000 to the purchase of seed, farming implements, and other things "necessary . . . for the commencement of farming."[15] In 1888 alone 3,568 allotments had been made.[16] The appropriation, therefore, granted less than ten dollars to every new allottee setting out on his farming career. There is, furthermore, no way of knowing how much of this money was expended for this purpose. However, it looked like the beginning of a policy and the Board of Indian Commissioners commended the Government for the step, while at the same time it hoped that in the future the appropriation would be increased.[17]

The following year the same amount was provided, but in 1890 no such appropriation was made. In 1891 Congress raised $15,000 for the purpose, and this sum was continued through the next two years.[18] After 1893 the appropriation acts up to 1900 included no such items. Agents' reports all through the period bear testimony to the sad needs of the Indians for material assistance in their farming. The agent to the Kiowas, Comanches, and Wichitas in 1890 wrote: "It is exceedingly hard to divide 115 plows among the three hundred odd Indians who declared they wanted to use them."[19] The Nevada agent wrote in 1892: "In a word, they are too poor to purchase tools to work with, and at present date have done nothing with the lands in consequence of their inability to buy necessary farming implements, etc."[20] This complaint is heard over and over again.[21] The failure of the Government to provide adequate equipment to the allottees was like its failure to provide vocational training. These omissions show the Government's inability to comprehend that the whole allotment program, if it was to succeed, should first of all have been an educational program which would realistically be concerned with the Indians' economic needs. But the Government had failed in these respects before. The Omaha treaties of 1854 and of 1868, which provided for a form of allotment, required the Government to furnish the Indians with implements, stock, and milling services.[22] Yet these promises were never carried out.[23] One of the Indians who signed the petition for the Omaha allotment bill in 1881 said: "Three times I have cut wood to build a house. Each time the agent told me the Government wished to build me a house. Every time my wood has lain and rotted, and now I feel ashamed when I hear an agent telling me such things."[24]

There were some attempts at private aid to the new American farmers. The largest venture seems to have been originated by Miss Fletcher and taken up by the Women's National Indian Association. It was a small-loan service to the Indians to help them build homes. In 1889 the president of the Association reported that several thousand dollars had been invested in this enterprise and in four years thirty or forty houses built.[25] But private philanthropy also proved entirely inadequate for the purpose of helping the Indians to make a go of allotment.

The reasons for this whole failure seem to be that in the first place most of the friends of the Indian showed a great lack of imagination and of any practical notion about what allotment for the Indian involved. They thought the law would work the transformation and would by definition make the Indian a farmer. All he then needed was Christianizing and culture. Therefore, in the second place, the law once passed, the friends of the Indian rested upon their laurels. They rested from thinking and toiling in behalf of the Indian, except when they were stirred by Senator Dawes, Miss Fletcher, and the other official leaders and convention goers. It is what happens to reform movements that pin their faith on legislation and finally achieve their laws. It happened to Indian reform as it happened to prohibition. Miss Anna L. Dawes, daughter of the Senator, said to the 1890 Mohonk Conference:

> I am quite sure that, while it is true that the interest of the country in the Indian and the sense of justice among the people at large is greatly increased and the

whole situation is better understood, it is also true that particular concrete interest is declining. At first it was a very glorious work. There were earnest public meetings and it was all quite exciting and very interesting. That time has passed by. With a few exceptions the work is no longer interesting. That does not seem true up here; but when we get home, we find the general public does not think or care very much about the Indians. The public cares little about details in the matter of help for the individual,—as to who has a house here, or a fence there, or a floor somewhere else. No one is willing to keep up the constant effort which is necessary to carry out such work.[26]

When vigilance in regard to a public issue declines in the democracy, it is the rule that Government will follow the line of least resistance. Therefore the ever-vigilant private interests swayed the Government in its policies. So Congress neglected to provide the funds adequately to carry out the allotment program, the Indian Administration attended to administration (and teaching the Indian "culture"), and about all that was given to the Indian was the freedom and American right to be exploited by shrewd white men.

A young Indian student at Yale addressed the 1889 Mohonk Conference in prophetic language. He said: "I believe, as has been said, that if the Indian takes up his land in severalty in the condition that he is now in, he will be worse off than if kept on the reservations. During these twenty-five years, the period of transition, the Indians are to be prepared for the duties of citizenship. Unless there is something done in that period, I think the Indians will be worse off than before."[27]

To eradicate the evils which they recognized in the allotment system the friends of the Indian characteristically turned to legislation again. In the first place, there was the very obvious need for civil service reform within the Indian department. Commissioner Morgan, who entered office in 1889, was especially hostile to the spoils system and determined to root it out of the Indian Service. General Armstrong said to the 1889 Mohonk Conference: "If the Commissioner can carry out his idea, he will be a 'bigger man than old Grant.' Let us back him up."[28] In 1889 and 1890 the Mohonk Conference adopted resolutions denouncing the spoils system and urging the President to extend civil service to all appointments made by the Indian Office.[29] The following year Herbert Welsh of the Indian Rights Association informed the conference that Indian agents could not be on the civil service list under existing law.[30] However, the conference expressed gratitude, in its resolution, for the fact that some 600 Indian Office employees had been brought under civil service, and it urged that the spirit of the law be applied to the appointment of Indian agents.[31] Thereafter the friends of allotment worked for changes in the law to make the agents civil service appointees, and by a series of laws the way was paved for the rather general removal of politics from the Indian Department shortly after 1900.[32]

Defects in the system which, in the second place, occupied the attention of the friends of the Indian were those resulting from the fact that allotted lands must be free from State taxation. The Dawes Act, providing for the twenty-five-year Federal trust period during which time the land might not be encumbered, meant, it was clear, that no State could tax the allottee's holdings. As a result, the friends of the Indian were noting in 1889, States were refusing to assume any responsibilities for Indian communities and were withholding such services as the upkeep of schools and roads. It was also apparent that this situation was a source of great hostility to Indians on the part of white neighbors.[33] The Mohonk Conference resolved in 1889 that the Federal Government should work out a system whereby funds from the sale of surplus lands should be turned over to States for the specific purposes of Indian education, in lieu of taxes.[34] Indian sympathizers continued to agitate this question through the 1890's.[35] There was at least one instance when the Federal Government adopted this policy which the friends of the Indian urged. In 1892 Congress passed a law reducing the Colville Reservation in the State of Washington. Section 2 provided that the Secretary of the Interior might use funds from the proceeds of the sale of surplus lands for the purposes of Indian education and "for the payment of such part of the local taxation as may be properly applied to the lands allotted to such Indians, as he shall think fit, so long as such allotted land shall be held in trust and exempt from taxation."[36] In 1926 and 1928 deficiency appropriation acts carried out the terms of this 1892 law by providing for the payment of sums to certain counties of Washington.[37] However, there was never any general legislation on the subject, nor did it become the practice of Congress to pass special laws of this sort. In fact, this act of 1892 relating to the Colville Indians is the only example which the writer has found of Federal grants to local governments in lieu of Indian taxes.[38]

In the third place, the most enthusiastic supporters of the allotment policy felt that its first results showed that it needed important revision itself. In his report for 1889 the Commissioner observed that Indians were asking for equal allotments to all individuals, and he recommended that the law should be so amended. He noted that there was a special need to protect the married women whom the Dawes Act had excluded from allotment benefits. The plight of the Indian wife was often desperate, since the husband, under the easy-going marriage system, might capriciously turn her out of his house and off his land.[39] Miss Fletcher was reported to favor the change to equal allotments for the same reason and for the reason that the existing differential was unwise and unjust in other ways. She pointed out that the Dawes Act gave 160 acres to the old and infirm and only forty acres to the young and able-bodied who were best qualified to work the land.[40] The Board of Indian Commissioners that same year urged upon Congress the equalization of allotments.[41]

This proposed change was, significantly, bound up with another and still more important change which most friends of the Indian came to demand. Professor Painter's dissertation to the 1889 Mohonk Conference on the Indian and his property stressed his theory that the Indian could not progress so long as he was hindered by the restrictions of the Dawes Act, especially by the restrictions on his economic liberty. The author favored giving the Indian the freedom to utilize his land to his best advantage.[42] The Mohonk Conference that year heard some talk about the leasing of Indian lands and the freeing of the Indian from bondage. Justice Strong, previously associate justice of the United States Supreme Court, said: "But on one subject I am perfectly convinced,—namely, that the government has not the shadow of a right to interfere with an Indian having an allotment, either with the use of his property or with the manner in which he shall educate his children . . . ."[43] But especially the point was emphasized that leasing part of his land would bring the Indian the wherewithal to cultivate the rest.[44] Other arguments from time to time were brought forward by Indian sympathizers to show how leasing would help him.

The Omaha and Winnebago agent in 1890 estimated that sixty percent of the Winnebago land belonged to women, or to the aged or to the very young—none of whom could cultivate his allotment. The agent also cited the case of students who were away at school and whose lands were lying unused and fallow. He argued that if all these persons were able to lease their holdings they would be supported by the rents therefrom. And he added a further and familiar argument: "Another feature, and by no means of the least importance, is the presence of good farmers, interspersed as they would be over the entire reservation, who would as object lessons be of incalculable value in teaching the principles of farming. This is not theory. We see the proof continually . . . . With a law constructed as I have indicated, I do not think idleness would be encouraged, and much good would result, and by leasing to small farmers for cultivation the pernicious practice of leasing large tracts to cattle men would be avoided."[45]

Indeed there was only one prophetic voice of warning raised against the leasing proposal, and that was Senator Dawes's. It is true that Professor Painter, while urging greater freedom for the Indian in the use of his property, had emphasized the evils of tribal grazing leases; but although he referred to these leases as deterrents from labor, he was mostly concerned with "the margin created by these lands about the Indian home" which served, "as did the old reservation, to shut out the industrious settler from a contact with the Indian which would help his education."[46] But Senator Dawes told the 1890 Mohonk Conference that a law which made it easy for the Indian to lease his land would frustrate all their hopes for the Indian's future. He said:

I know there are instances of hardship under this inalienable allotment system, and instances of worthy young men who want to leave their allotment and go into some other business or get an education; and in an endeavor to meet those cases we are in danger of overthrowing the fundamental idea of the whole system, that controlling idea that work on one's own homestead is the most potent of all civilizing agencies for the Indians. We are trying to meet these exceptional cases by permitting the allottee to leave his land when the agent or the Secretary, or some one else, "may deem it for his advantage so to do." In all this we forget that the Indian, as a rule, won't work if he can help it, and that the white has never been known to take his foot off from an Indian's land, when he once got it on. A bill has already passed the House, and is now pending in the Senate, authorizing the leasing of allotted lands whenever the agent shall deem it best for the Indian. Such a law, in my opinion, would speedily overthrow the whole allotment system. The Indian would at once seek to let his land, and relieve himself from work; and there would be whites so ready to take possession that all barriers would soon be broken down. Thus the allotment law would be gradually undermined and destroyed, and the Indian would abandon his own work, his own land, and his own home, which we have talked about as the central pivot of our efforts in attempting to civilize the Indian.[47]

But the legislative committee of the Mohonk Conference that year gave a report on the bill pending in Congress which provided for the granting of allotments to Indian married women, the guaranteeing of inheritance to the issue of Indian marriages, and for the leasing of allotments.

The committee said, "We are of opinion that these are measures of great importance, and our representatives in Congress should be urged to pass these bills without delay."[48] The Conference unanimously adopted a resolution which read, "That Congress be urged not to abrogate the twenty-five-year postponement of power to convey or contract away lands, any further than by a guarded power to lease on cause being shown, such as is contained in Senate Bill 3043."[49] Likewise, the Indian Rights Association, in its report for the year 1890, urged the adoption of the pending measure.[50]

The decision to allow the Indian to lease his land was fraught with grave consequences for the whole allotment system. Probably it was the most important decision as to Indian policy that was made after the passage of the Dawes Act. Yet, interestingly enough, the significance of the leasing question seemed to be dwarfed in the eyes of contemporaries by the pressing matter of equal allotments. It is true that after the Attorney General ruled in 1885 that tribal grazing leases were illegal, the Commissioner of Indian Affairs recommended annually until 1889 a law permitting such leases.[51] But he made no proposal of leasing allotments. And no doubt his advocating the grazing leases was looked at with suspicion by the friends of the Indian, as were most of his official acts.[52]

The question of leasing allotments had been raised at the 1889 Mohonk Conference,[53] but the Indian Office took no stand on the question in that year. As had been said, Commissioner Morgan was interested in the question of granting equal allotments to Indians of all ages and both sexes.[54] In January, 1890, he wrote a letter to the Secretary of the Interior enclosing a bill providing for the granting of 160 acres to every Indian—man, woman, and child. The

following month the President transmitted the bill, together with Commissioner Morgan's letter to the Senate
Committee on Indian Affairs. The Commissioner mentioned several tribes which had opposed allotment because
they disliked the system of unequal grants to the different
classifications and he thought that if 160 acres were given
each Indian "there would be less hesitation on the part of
many of the tribes to the taking of land in severalty." He
also stressed the predicament of cast-off Indian wives under
the existing system and the importance of dealing more
liberally with the young Indians who were the future hope
of the race.[55]

Accordingly, on March 10, 1890, Senator Dawes introduced in the Senate a bill to "amend and further extend
the benefits" of the Dawes Act.[56] Section 1 of the bill provided for the granting of 160 acres to every Indian. The
previous agitation of this question by the official and unof-
ficial friends of the Indian furnished an adequate introduction to this legislative proposal. But Section 2 of the bill
seems to have come almost unheralded from Senator
Dawes, the man who a few months later publicly expressed
his misgivings about the leasing policy.[57] Section 2 of the
Senator's bill read:

> That whenever it shall be made to appear to the Secre-
> tary of the Interior that, by reason of age or other disa-
> bility, any allottee under the provisions of said act or any
> other act or treaty cannot personally and with benefit to
> himself occupy or improve his allotment, or any part
> thereof, the same may be leased upon such terms, regu-
> lations, and conditions as shall be prescribed by said Sec-
> retary, for a term not exceeding three years for farming
> or grazing, or ten years for mining purposes.[58]

Section 3 legitimatized the descendants of Indian parents

who had cohabited according to Indian custom. After being referred to the Indian Affairs Committee, the bill was amended by the committee to grant eighty acres to every Indian married woman instead of 160 acres to each Indian, and to extend the benefits of Section 3 to all mixed-bloods. Section 2 was left entirely as it had been when first introduced by Senator Dawes.[59] On April 23 the bill, as reported by the committee, was engrossed, read for the third time, and passed by the Senate without debate. The House Committee on Indian Affairs promptly amended the Senate bill.[60] The committee changed Section 1 so as to allot eighty acres to every Indian, and it changed Section 2 to read: "That whenever it shall be made to appear to the agent in charge of any reservation Indians that, by reason of age or any other sufficient cause," an allottee could not utilize his allotment he could lease his lands subject to the approval of the Secretary for as long as five years in the case of farming or grazing or ten years in the case of mining lands.[61] Thus it was to be made easy for an Indian to become a landlord. On September 29 the House turned its attention to this bill for a few minutes. One member asked to have clarified the phrase "nonresident Indian"; and then, without further debate, the House passed the amended bill. The Senate disagreed to the House amendments, but a conference committee reached a compromise which was accepted by both Senate and House on February 23, 1891.[62] Eighty acres were to go to each Indian, but an Indian could rent his land only when unable to work it "by reason of age or other disability." The Indian must apply for a lease to the Secretary of the Interior directly and not to the agent, and farming and grazing leases of allotted lands could be for no longer than three years.[63] In other words, there was to be something in the way of restraint exercised upon Indian leasing. The President signed the bill on February 28, 1891.

Again one is impressed by the lack of interest shown in the leasing question, even among the legislators. There was not one word of debate in either house on the leasing provisions of the bill, nor for that matter was there any real debate on any part of the measure. The only interest shown was in the question as to whether each Indian should get eighty or 160 acres. Chairman Bishop W. Perkins of the House Committee said representatives of the Board of Indian Commissioners and of the Indian Rights Association were urging passage of the bill but were mostly indifferent as to which of the two acreages was allotted.[64] The committee report on the original House bill included a letter from a former special Indian agent and statements by General Whittlesey of the Board of Indian Commissioners and Professor Painter, national lobbyist for the Indian Rights Association. These gentlemen all urged the need of equalizing allotments, and Professor Painter mentioned the importance of enabling the Indian "to use" his land, but none of them discussed the leasing question. They all, however, endorsed the House bill.[65] Indeed, the Indian Rights Association preferred the House bill, with its more liberal leasing policy, to the original Senate measure. The Association liked the phrase "or any other sufficient cause," since it would permit women and students away at school to rent their lands.[66] The Commissioner observed in 1890 that the Senate proposal to give eighty acres only to married women did not touch the basic problem of equality. He noted also that the Senate had added measures for leasing allotments and for legitimizing Indian offspring. He gave both provisions his blessing, especially the latter provision.[67] The 1891 Mohonk Conference resolved that the year had been most fruitful in legislation; and the resolutions listed several enactments of Congress, but the act of February 28 was not numbered among them.[68] The annual report of the Indian Rights Association for 1891 made no comment on the new law.[69]

Because of this apparent prevailing indifference and lack of contention as regards the leasing question it is difficult to form any very clear idea as to the origin of the policy. However the western land-seekers and business interests felt about the original allotment policy, it was obvious that the leasing of Indian lands was entirely favorable to their interests. No opposition to the leasing project in Congress could be looked for in that quarter. As in the case of the allotment policy, there is no evidence to show that white westerners formulated the new program. However, a demand for the leasing of Indian lands could have come quite naturally and spontaneously from western communities. White men saw before them fertile Indian acres now in the hands of individual owners. For the most part these Indian owners were not active farmers who made the most of their lands. On the other hand, they were always tractable in money matters and would be very willing to rent—if the Government would let them. What would be more natural, then, for ambitious settlers and entrepreneurs to apply to the Government for its consent to their developing lands which would otherwise be idle and wasted? Whatever the western white had to do with originating the leasing policy, it is inconceivable that he did not help the policy forward.

In general, the philanthropists seem to have favored leasing, although not with the same enthusiasm that marked their interest in allotment. After all, leasing did not appear to be an exciting and drastic change of policy. It was another and strictly logical stage in the development of the principle underlying allotment. The arguments of Professor Painter about the Indian and his property appealed to the friends of the Indian: What was the use of making the Indian a responsible individual if you did not give him the freedom to go ahead? How could he go ahead in the world if he could not have free use of his property? The cure for the ills of freedom was more freedom. Senator Dawes, the most clear-headed of the friends of the Indian, would not blind himself to the dangers of allowing the Indian to lease his lands. He painted those dangers in vivid colors to the Mohonk Conference in 1890.[70] Yet seven months before he had put forward his leasing bill in Congress. In 1891 the Senator told the Mohonk Conference that he had previously been opposed to the leasing idea but he had seen the Indians so often grow discouraged in their attempts to break the prairie lands that he concluded it would be wise to let the Indians rent parts of their lands. Thus the owners would have funds to develop their remaining acres while the rented portions would be improved by the lessees. But the Senator warned that the policy must be carefully administered.[71] There was, however, one voice raised against the leasing system. In 1892 the Sac and Fox agent wrote from Oklahoma:

Should authority be given for the Indians to lease their lands, nearly all would avail themselves of the privilege and their land would be immediately taken up by whites (probably for subleasing purposes) at ridiculously low compensation and the Indian would squander the proceeds and still live an idle, vagabond life. The average Indian is not competent to make leases and care for his own interest. As it would require constant watchfulness

115

to protect him from imposition, I consider that leasing would be detrimental, and that the land would soon become impoverished . . . .

There have been no leases made by authority at this agency.[72]

On the other hand, several agents expressed decided approval of the new leasing policy, although they usually agreed that the term of three years for agricultural leases was too short a time to attract the right sort of lessee. They recommended that the period be extended to five or even ten years.[73]

One of the agents expressed more or less adequately the complex of motives which were behind the leasing policy. The Santee agent wrote concerning leasing in 1892: "It would seem probable to me that it might give the Indian more idea as to the value of land to see others making use of it, and be also a source of income for himself, and it certainly would be a source of gratification to the whites to see the land in use instead of lying idle."[74]

The Indian Administration set out at a very cautious gait to apply the leasing provision to allotments. The Commissioner in his report for 1892 said: "Agents are expressly directed that it is not intended to authorize the making of any lease by an allottee who possesses the necessary physical and mental qualifications to enable him to cultivate his allotment, either personally or by hired help."[75] He said that but two allotment leases had thus far been approved by him.[76] The next year the Commissioner promulgated a set of rules for the making of leases. The rules were primarily concerned with defining the terms in the phrase, "by reason of age or other disability." "Age" applied to all Indians under eighteen and all those disabled by senility. "Other disability" applied to all unmarried Indian women, married women whose husband or sons were unable to work the land, widows without able-bodied sons, all Indians with chronic sickness or incurable physical defect, and those with "native defect of mind or permanent incurable mental disease."[77] The Commissioner reported that four allotment leases had been allowed that year.[78] However, the Commissioner made one remark which indicated that he did not regard as important in administration one of the safeguards which Senator Dawes had insisted on. The Senator had secured an amendment to the House bill taking away from the agents the power of recommending leases and requiring the Indians to apply directly to the Secretary of the Interior.[79] But in 1893 the Commissioner wrote: "The matter of leasing allotted lands has been placed largely in the hands of the Indian agents in charge of the agencies where allotments in severalty have been made." He went on to say that all leases must be approved by the Secretary after recommendation by the agent.[80] How much this administrative ruling was in itself responsible for the subsequent speeding-up of leasing cannot be said, for at that point a most important change was made in the law. Apparently those who were in favor of the leasing policy were coming to the conclusion that one could not have too much of a good thing. They were perhaps influenced by such hopeful arguments as that put forward by the agent to the Cheyennes and Arapahoes in 1894. He wrote:

As the average number in each family is about five, it will readily be seen that when they are required to make their homes upon one allotment, and the remaining four leased to white men who would cultivate the same on shares, that the portion due the Indian family would be more than actually required for subsistence, and that each year they would have a surplus to sell, the proceeds of which could be invested in stock or improvements on the home tract.[81]

At any rate, the general Indian appropriation act, which became law August 15, 1894, contained a provision which changed the critical phrase in the act of 1891 to read "by reason of age, disability or inability," extended the term of agricultural and grazing leases to five years and permitted ten-year leases for business as well as mining purposes.[82] Nevertheless, the Commissioner said in his report that year: "It has been repeatedly stated that it was not the intent of the law nor the policy of the office to allow indiscriminate leasing of allotted lands . . . . If an allottee has physical or mental ability to cultivate an allotment by personal labor or by hired help, the leasing of such allotment should not be permitted."[83] But a new rule which the Commissioner added to those defining "age" and "disability" read: "The term 'inability' as used in said amended act, cannot be specifically defined as the other terms have been. Any allottee not embraced in any of the foregoing classes who for any reason other than those stated is unable to cultivate his lands or a portion of them, and desires to lease same, may make application therefor to the proper Indian agent."[84]

The Board of Indian Commissioners, reporting early in 1895, made note of the change in the leasing law and expressed its gratification that the Commissioner had avowed his intention to see that no capable Indian should be allowed to lease his allotment. Nevertheless, the Board pointed out, there had been 295 leases of allotments approved in 1894 (as contrasted with four in 1893 and two in 1892). The Board was alarmed at the trend.[85] Outright dismay was expressed at the 1894 Mohonk Conference at the direction in which the leasing policy was carrying them. Professor Painter said that the original aims of the allotment system had been to give lands to those who were prepared to receive them; then to secure these lands by the twenty-five-year clause so that the young might be educated to make use of them; and finally to modify the system to allow those who could not use lands to lease them. He concluded: "I wish to call attention to the fact that in all three of these particulars the principle of the bill, the spirit and intent of the bill, are being set aside and destroyed."[86] Significantly, he went on to suggest what the forces were that were promoting the changes in the system. He said: "We have reached a crisis. It is the intention of men in the West, and their efforts are being more and more felt in Congress as the power of the West is becoming greater in controlling national affairs,—it is the intention of these men to sweep away all these limitations and restrictions which the severalty law put in the Indian's power to alienate his land."[87] The platform of the Conference that year stated: "Recent laws permitting Indians to lease their lands are widely resulting in dispossessing ignorant Indians of their property rights, without an adequate return, to their great disadvantage and the enriching of designing white men."[88]

The Indian Rights Association in its 1894 report vigorously assailed the course which the Government was following. After denouncing the relaxation of restrictions upon leasing and upon even the sale of Indian allotments, the report concluded: "It cannot be said too strongly or urgently that attention should be aroused, and intelligent action at once taken, or the severalty law will prove as unavailing as treaties have been to protect the Indian in the possession of his land."[89] Apparently one could have too much of a good thing after all.

The Commissioner on his part continued to declare that his purpose held to see that Indians who could farm their lands were not allowed to lease them.[90] The Board of Indian Commissioners in 1895 were pleased that the Commissioner took this stand, but even so they thought there should be legislative changes to restrict allotment leases.[91] If the Commissioner's rule was regularly applied, it became clear that either the Indians were growing more incompetent or more incompetent Indians were being discovered, for leasing increased by leaps and bounds. From 295 leases of allotments in 1894, the number grew to 330 in 1895, to 933 in 1896, and 1,287 in 1897.[92] There was little said about this development. For the most part from 1895 on the friends of the Indian busied themselves with such questions as improving the service, prohibiting the sale of liquor to the Indians, reorganizing the Indian Administration, and extending the allotment system to the Five Civilized Tribes.

The reports of the Board of Indian Commissioners, the Indian Rights Association, and the Mohonk Conference expressed little concern with the leasing question, although a faith in allotment was continually reaffirmed. Nevertheless, the Indian Appropriation Act of 1897 changed the leasing system back to its original form. Indeed in one respect the provisions were even more restrictive than were those of the 1891 law. The maximum term for mining and business leases was fixed at five years. The term for farming and grazing leases was changed back to three years and the word "inability" was dropped so that "age or other disability" became the only legal grounds for permitting leases.[93] The Commissioner's report for 1897 commented on the fact that the leasing periods had been changed by the Indian appropriation act but, interestingly enough, he made no mention of the dropping of the word "inability."[94] The 1894 reports of the various societies of Indian sympathizers seemed to regard the leasing changes not important enough to mention, although the publication of the Indian Rights Association discussed other features of the appropriation act.[95] Whether or not the legislative changes were responsible for it, a slight change in policy was reflected in the number of leases that were approved in 1898. The figure dropped to 948 as compared with 1,287 in the preceding year.[96] But at once enthusiasm for Indian leasing was rekindled. The Commissioner approved 1,185 allotment leases in 1899, and 2,500 in 1900.[97] In this latter year, the system was again changed by the Indian appropriation act. "Inability" was restored as a reason for permitting allotment leases, and the maximum period of leasing for farming purposes was extended once more to five years.[98] These changes were denounced by the friends of the Indian. The Board of Indian Commissioners, the Mohonk Conference, and the Indian Rights Association in 1900 severally deplored the new policy as encouraging the pauperizing and general demoralization of the Indian.[99]

Apparently the change in policy had not been the doing of the Commissioner. He wrote in his report for 1900:

> The better to assist them the allottees should be divided into small communities, each to be put in charge of persons who by precept and example would teach them how to work and how to live.
>
> This is the theory. The practice is very different. The Indian is allotted and then allowed to turn over his land to the whites and go on his aimless way. This pernicious practice is the direct growth of vicious legislation. The first law on the subject was passed in 1891 . . . .

THE DAWES ACT

It is conceded that where an Indian allottee is incapac-
itated by physical disability or decrepitude of age from
occupying and working his allotment, it is proper to permit him to lease it, and it was to meet such cases as this
that the law referred to was made . . . . But "inability"
has opened the door for leasing in general, until on some
of the reservations leasing is the rule and not the exception, while on others the practice is growing . . . .

To the thoughtful mind it is apparent that the effect
of the general leasing of allotments is bad. Like the gra-
tuitous issue of rations and the periodical distribution of
money it fosters indolence with its train of attendant
vices. By taking away the incentive to labor it defeats
the very object for which the allotment system was devised, which was, by giving the Indian something tangible
that he could call his own, to incite him to personal effort
in his own behalf.[100]

Thus it seems that the leasing policy had been pushed
much further than the friends of the Indian desired. As to
who had been pushing it there one can only guess. It is
apparent that white settlers and promoters had found leasing a new and effective technique for exploiting Indian
lands. So had Indian agents—according to the Indian
Rights Association. The Association's report for 1900 described the evil consequences of the leasing system under
the new law and set forth grave charges:

It will readily be seen that with a liberal construction
of this statute any Indian allotment can legally be leased,
and we find that at all agencies the practice of leasing is
a growing evil; the allottee becomes discouraged, leases
his lands, and usually his house, built for him often partly
at Government expense, and retires to the life of the
camp. The leasing is usually encouraged by the agents or
others having charge of the Indians for profit only, since it

can easily be made a source of considerable income. The would-be renter seeks the agent having charge of the lands, makes an inferior offer of the rents of certain allotments, and agrees to pay the agent a stipulated bonus if he will recommend that the lease be made. Where many thousand acres are available for leasing, the income to the agent from this source might many times exceed his salary.[101]

# CHAPTER IX

## RESULTS OF ALLOTMENT
## TO 1900

Analysis of the achievements of the allotment system requires first some appraisal of the leasing practice which vitally affected allotment results. There were defenders of the leasing system all through the 1890's. It had certain immediate consequences which recommended it to friends of the Indian, who were sincere if lacking in vision. There was the simple fact of allotted lands lying idle which the Indians either could not or would not cultivate. Such waste seemed wicked to a generation that was coming increasingly to set store by efficiency. How much better it was for the lands to be used and the Indians to be deriving an income from them. In 1890, before the passage of the leasing act, a member of the Board of Indian Commissioners regretted that the Government had ousted white share workers from the Kiowa, Comanche, and Apache reservations. He said: "Farms that could only be worked in this way, owing to peculiar circumstances, are now lying tenantless and abandoned."[1] In 1895 various agents expressed their approval of the way leasing was working, since it was bringing in to the Indians a sizeable revenue.[2] In 1898 the Sac and Fox agent in Oklahoma found that this benefit of leasing coincided even with an educational value. He wrote: "About one-half of their lands are leased and with the best of results, as a source of revenue to the allottee, and his contact with the white lessees is encouraging more of them to work themselves."[3] One would like to know whether the Indians' inspired ambitions led them to reclaim the other half of their lands from their teachers. But it was frequently insisted that leasing had wholesome educational results, although these results were never very explicitly described as having already made themselves apparent. The Sisseton agent wrote in 1895: "I have not interfered or discouraged them in leasing their surplus land under such contracts for the reason that I believe it will aid them in their progress for independent action at some future time. It adds to their experience in doing business for themselves."[4]

But for the most part, the agents who expressed their approval of allotment leasing saw it as productive of practical results. It took care of minors, women, and the old folks,[5] and it was economically profitable. One agent said the Indians got more out of the leased lands than if they worked them themselves.[6] This last comment forbode ill for the allotment system. The Sac and Fox agent who in 1898 saw the leasing practice as an educational venture wrote two years before: "Those Indians who have refused to take their allotments have begun to realize what benefits accrue to those who have accepted them from the leasing system."[7] Leasing was undoubtedly a spur to the taking of allotments. But it seems hardly to have been a spur to the Indian becoming a farmer. Perhaps some Indian lessors learned the doctrine of hard work from their white tenants. But evidence seems to show that what they learned mostly was to reap where they did not sow.

The agent to the Tonkawas wrote in 1894: "These Indians have all taken their land in severalty, and are anxious that their allotments shall be improved. They manifest this desire, however, more by the readiness to lease to white men than by diligent labor to improve their own homes."[8] The threat that this tendency made to the allotment system was clearly foreseen by Senator Dawes when he warned the 1890 Mohonk Conference of the dangers of leasing. He told of Indians whom he had known in Indian Territory who had been completely demoralized by the practice of allowing white men to work their lands on shares. The Senator concluded by saying: "The Indians outside the Territory have acquired this passion for giving up their land for money in hand. The allotment law, which had its origin in the idea that work on the soil was the one thing of all others necessary to civilize the Indian, is in danger of being itself undermined by this attempt to lease the land which the allotment compels them to occupy for twenty-five years."[9] But as has been shown above, the Indian Administration was unable to work out effective checks upon the leasing policy to prevent its running to extremes. And Congress, but for the brief hope of restraint it offered by the act of 1897, seemed willing to let the Indian go his own sweet way in the real estate business.

The Potawatomi and Great Nemaha agent wrote in 1898: "Their lands are leased to a very large extent with discouraging and dangerous results. As at first proposed, the ill results might have been checked, but with the numerous modifications that have been adopted an agency is becoming a machine through which large sums of money are disbursed to immoral, dissipated, and utterly thoughtless persons, who have neither occasion nor disposition to resort to labor, and many of whom are without moral perception."[10]

At the end of the century the Board of Indian Commissioners said, "We take note of the fact that there is a growing tendency on the part of allotted Indians at certain reservations to look at their individual allotments of land, not as homesteads on which work is to be done for the support of the family, but only as property to be leased in order that the Indian who owns it may live without work upon his income from rent."[11] And the outspoken opinion of the Commissioner of Indian Affairs in 1900 has already been recorded.[12]

The Sac and Fox agency seemed to hold true to its faith in leasing as a civilizing process.[13] The Quapaw agent started out with the same faith. In 1894 he thought the white tenants had "done wonders toward civilizing the Indians."[14] In 1895 he saw the civilized millenium opening up for his Indians. He wrote:

A few months ago there was nothing at Wyandotte but a post-office and a few houses. Now, since the leases have been approved, quite an impetus has been given to the town, and what with ground being broken for business buildings, bank buildings, schoolhouses, and churches of most all denominations, the town in a few years will put on the garb of an incorporated city . . . .

The white laborers, or lessees, on this reservation, from the best information that I am able to get, will number about 5,000, and the majority of them are here through the solicitation of the Indians . . . . Through them the Indians learn that this is a country of free thought and free speech; that this is an age of self-endeavor, of advancement, and of growth; that the old custom must give way to a new order of affairs. The above can truly be said of the conscientious white settler and not be called "rose-colored."[15]

Whether or not this estimate could be called "rose-colored," the Indians were very soon given a lesson in free thought, free speech, and self-endeavor. In 1896 the agent had to report that he had gone after those whites who had illegal leases, and finally ordered them off the reservation. But those free American citizens held meetings, defied the agent, threatened his life, and were on the point of storming the agency when wiser counsel prevailed. He was finally able to expel twenty-four lessees and 300 others left rather than abide by the leasing rules.[16] This incident certainly had something to teach the Indian about civilization.

Perhaps the most flagrant example of the corrosive influence of leasing was that of the Omahas and Winnebagoes, in Nebraska. The Omahas were the great hope of the allotment enthusiasts. But in 1893 the agent wrote that leasing had gone far among the Omahas and Winnebagoes and that the former were renting their lands without the consent of the agent or Government.[17] In 1894 the Indian Rights Association reported, "Recent investigations among the Omahas reveal the fact that only a very few of these allottees, formerly sober, industrious, and progressive, who made a most hopeful beginning immediately after their lands were given them in severalty, are now living in their houses or cultivating their land. White men, who never expect to relax their hold, occupy them, and the Indians, for the most part, are in camps along the Missouri River, dancing and carousing." The Association pointed out that as a result of the most recent law anyone unable to cultivate his land "for lack of ponies or for whatever reason" could lease his allotment.[18] That year, 1894, Professor Painter told the Mohonk Conference of his bitter disappointment in the Omahas especially, about whom he had been satisfied and enthusiastic as they had started out under the allotment system. He had recently visited the two reservations and found most of the land in white hands. Real estate syndicates had leased lands even before the allotment was completed. One company had rented 47,000 acres from the Winnebagoes at from eight to ten to twenty-five cents an acre and sublet to white farmers for one to two dollars an acre. The Winnebagoes got enough income from these lands to stay drunk part of the time. But the Omahas got much more.[19]

The illegal leasing of allotments had apparently gone to great lengths on these two reservations.[20] In 1894 the agent thought that the Indians were anxious to recover their lands and till some portion of them.[21] The following year this fighting agent set out in a vain effort to bring to heel a powerful land company. The Government ultimately furnished him with fifty extra police and seventy rifles as the local authorities rallied to the support of the land company and were reported to be arming a hundred deputies. Confronted by an injunction in the State courts restraining him from evicting the company's tenants, the agent at last gave in.[22] In 1894 the agent had written, "The settlers would almost unanimously prefer to lease under the rules and regulations of the Department; but are held, pecuniarily, by the lawless corporations and individuals who have subleased to them."[23] In 1895 the Commissioner explained the effective technique of this particular land company which had been able to flout the Federal authority. His explanation suggests very clearly why this outlaw corporation received the community's support. In many instances the company accepted notes from their subtenants in place of money rent. These notes in turn came into the hands of local bankers. As a result all of the powerful interests in the community were galvanized in opposition to the Government in its attempt to force evictions or collect legal rents.[24]

Whatever progress the Omahas, especially, might have made under the original allotment system, it is clear that the leasing policy doomed their efforts to failure and themselves to demoralization. A modern anthropologist, who recently made an exhaustive study of the Omahas, wrote, "Never properly accustomed to farming, not yet sufficiently good farmers to make an income very superior, or half so reliable as the rent from a white tenant, two-thirds of the Indian men ceased to make any further economic struggle . . . . There was no incentive to improving a standard of living already so alien to them."[25]

The passionate denunciation of leasing by the Omaha and Winnebago agent in 1898 perhaps says the last word on the matter. He wrote that out of 140,000 acres allotted on the two reservations, 112,000 acres had been leased. He then wrote:

> Leasing of allotted agricultural lands should never be permitted. The Indians should be compelled to live upon their allotments and support themselves by cultivating the land. They can do it, but will not unless compelled to. Not one acre of allotted agricultural land should be leased to a white man, and it would be far better to burn the grass on the allotted lands than to lease them for pastures to the white man. The Indians could use them to advantage for stock raising if they would. The mixing of the Indians with the class of whites who live upon and hang around an Indian reservation means the production of a mongrel race, embodying all of the vices and none of the virtues of the dominant race; it means death industrially, morally, and physically to the Indian. Not a white man should be allowed within the limits of the

reservation until the Government has so far advanced the Indian, by compulsion if necessary, in the industries of his reservation that they are a self-supporting community and all business and trades conducted by them. If they are to be allowed to mix, let the Indians go among the whites—not the whites among the Indians—and he will then meet them as an independent, self-supporting individual, capable, through proper instruction, to transact his own business as between man and man and with the better class of whites; not as now, as an ignoramus in the hands of unprincipled sharpers . . . .

What a revelation it would be to our Mr. Indian if he could travel in the plane of average honor and virtue of the white man, instead of being forever brought in touch with the level of maximum vice, fraud, and deceit of the white race.[26]

Yet in 1892 Miss Alice C. Fletcher had said of the Omahas, "The people are learning by the best of teachers, experience."[27] Miss Fletcher never lost her faith in the progress of the Omahas under allotment. As late as 1910 she returned to the reservation and the things that she saw reaffirmed her belief that the Omahas were on the right road.[28] Yet most of the evidence from the 1890's and the most recent analysis of the community piece together a picture of a demoralized people.

It is difficult indeed to make a complete generalization about the results of the whole allotment policy as they manifested themselves by 1900. As before the passage of the Dawes Act there is conflicting testimony and one must constantly sift and evaluate before one can render a verdict. Particularly is it hard to give a verdict when certain unknown persons among the star witnesses are under suspicion of being parties interested in the case. Most of the direct testimony as to the results of the allotment policy comes from the Indian agents. The serious charges preferred against some of the agents by the Indian Rights Association in 1900 —that they connived with land sharks in leasing transactions—makes the reader deal cautiously with all agents' reports.

The agents' reports from 1887 to 1900 continued to express approval and gratification about the allotment system. Indians were constantly being reported to be improving in their farming technique and interest. The Commissioner reported in 1891 that allotment had been pushed with "unusual vigor" that year and that the Indians were receiving their allotments with increasing favor.[29] In 1892 he sent out a questionnaire to all agents inquiring as to progress and received enthusiastic replies about allotment as a civilizing agent.[30] But the agents gave little specific information. In 1898 and 1899 the Board of Indian Commissioners circularized the agents with more specific questions. Again the agents pretty generally expressed their approval of allotment results. In the few cases where the agents believed the system had not been so successful they explained that the soil was not adapted to farming or that drouths had interfered.[31] But there is a disturbing vagueness about most of their replies. Indeed their reassuring general statements were often vitiated by some of their specific items of information.

Some excerpts from the answers to the questionnaire of 1898 will serve as examples. The Sac and Fox agent in Oklahoma wrote, "The benefits to the Indian in taking his allotment are numerous. It brings him more directly in contact with civilization. He observes more closely the advantages of industry and frugality as seen in his white neighbors. He is brought face to face with the advantages of education, sobriety, and religious habits of life." He then stated that not over one-fifth of his Indians cultivated their lands.[32] The agent to the Nez Perces wrote that four-fifths of his Indians were living on their allotments. But he said that only ten percent of the land was cultivated and even on these lands the Indians hired white men "to do most of the work." But the agent thought the allotment system had great benefits. "It gives the Indian a chance to be a man among men . . . . The allotment policy, if carried to a finish, will also work a hardship on my friend Cody, by soon depriving him of suitable material for his 'Wild West' shows."[33] The Lower Brule agent said his Indians cultivated the soil "to a very limited extent" for it was a very poor farming country. But he said, "In my opinion it is a great benefit to the Indians to allot them land in severalty, as it has a tendency to scatter them out from their camps and make them individually responsible for their own property."[34] The agent of the Poncas, Pawnees, and Tonkawas believed allotment was a great thing for the Indians. He thought the "benefits are numerous and the evils few." Yet he informed the Board that the Poncas were cultivating 1,500 acres and leasing 30,000; the Pawnees were cultivating 1,443 acres and leasing 36,784; and the Tonkawas cultivated 75 acres and leased 11,200.[35] If this agent thought that in such a situation the benefits were numerous and the evils few, he clearly did not grasp Senator Dawes's original conception of allotment. If the success of the allotment system was to be measured in terms of the prosperity that came through rents to idle but civilized Indians, then the whole notion of the allotment policy had changed since the early days.

However, certain answers to the questionnaires of 1898 and 1899, together with various regular reports of agents through the period, indicated that allotment was successful in all respects in the industrial, as well as the cultural, progress of the Indians. Usually these statements were very general, but, again, they sometimes included specific information which supported the agents' eulogies of the allotment system's results.[36] There is no reason to doubt that there were instances where allotment was working well.

On the other hand agents now and then reported that allotment had signally failed. Few of the replies to the questionnaires of 1898 and 1899 explicitly reported failures, and when they did, they usually included remarks attributing any shortcomings in the system to local, or at least particularized causes, which could be eradicated. The statement of the Devils Lake agent in 1898 is typical of these replies. He wrote:

> The benefits of the allotment system are, first, a wider knowledge of individual property rights, consequently some degree of personal responsibility (though the latter is not a marked feature of the present generation on this reservation); second, a tendency to fixed habitation and home building; the evils seem to arise from ignorance on their part and the selection, in many instances, of lands totally unfitted to agriculture; third [sic], dividing the allotments in 40-acre lots, in some instances many miles apart, necessitating great inconvenience in the cultivation; fourth, allotting to children should be discontinued, the land being saved and allotted when the child becomes of age and has saved enough to cultivate it.[37]

In answer to the questionnaire of 1899 many agents urged the abandonment of the exclusively agricultural policy of the allotment system with the implication that it had not succeeded. They advocated in its place the development of cattle raising.[38] In 1898 the Crow Creek agent, however, noting the failure of Indian agriculture on his reservation, regretted the lack of cattle raising in words which challenged the very basis of the allotment system. He wrote, "But if these people could have been given a sufficient number of cattle to start a common herd among them, and the reservation fenced, I think they would have been in a much better condition now . . . ."[39] The Omaha and Winnebago agent, as he inveighed against the leasing system, wrote also in 1898: "The allotment of agricultural lands to Indians as at present made is a mistaken policy. If the Indians have a reservation of agricultural lands it should be kept in its tribal form for purposes of control, government, and isolation from disreputable whites. It should be apportioned in uniformly suitable tracts in size, locality, etc., for future allotment."[40] According to most of the reports of the agents through the nineties the Omaha allotment system, from which so much was originally hoped, was spelling ruin and demoralization.[41]

The Tulalip agent could say nothing good of allotment in 1895. He wrote:

> . . . there are a large number of Indians holding patents to land who do not live on their lands, never made any improvements—indeed, some do not know exactly where their lands are, while others do not live on a reservation and have been absent for several years. The only practical effect of such a policy is, under the allotment act of 1887, as construed by the courts in the West, to thrust citizenship upon the Indians when they are, as a rule, totally unprepared and unfit to discharge the obligations imposed upon them. The Indian is quick, however, to avail himself of one of the inalienable rights of American citizenship, and gets gloriously drunk, having no dread of punishment by Indian courts or agent to mar the pleasure of his debauch.[42]

The agent to the Cheyennes and Arapahoes in 1895 was finding that the familiar Indian cultural patterns were obstructing the allotment policy and the development of the proprietary sense. He wrote:

> It has required energy and perseverence to induce settlement and permanent residence thereon. Their nomadic habits militate against the permanent occupation of any locality as a home . . . . To live in one locality is repugnant to the Indian idea of home. That they must have a permanent abiding place in order to make any sort of progress is evident. They must learn to cultivate a love of individual ownership. Property in common is not appreciated.
>
> The most common and pernicious custom among them is the habit of visiting their relatives and friends and eating their substance . . . . Their lavish hospitality militates against the accumulation of wealth by individuals. Tribal visiting keeps alive old customs and should be abolished.[43]

Agents who expressed faith in the allotment system as the solution of the Indian's problem found this inertia of tribal economy most annoying. The Shoshone agent wrote in 1891: "Like all barbarians, they are communists, and are loath to take up individually any untried pursuit. There are a few in each tribe who, with a little assistance, would soon develop into excellent farmers."[44] The agent to the Otoes found them bitterly opposing allotment in 1895. He wrote: "This way of living in camps should be broken up in some way, and I believe the proper means to obtain abandonment of all these evils is to segregate them and force them, if necessary, to a separate residence on their allotments."[45] Yet one agent apparently did not believe that this adherence to an older economy on the part of the Indians was always productive of evil. He wrote in 1892 concerning one band of the Sac and Fox: "They live in groups, breaking and cultivating land without regard to individual ownership. Yet I must say that this band is above the average for sobriety, honesty, industry, and thrift, notwithstanding their determination not to follow the ways of the white man."[46]

Again it should be said that it is difficult to make a final estimate of the results of allotment in the nineties on the basis of available testimony, which is for the most part testimony of agents and other interested persons. If the agents' general comments could be accepted at their face value, the success of allotment up to 1900 could be considered proven. But, as was said above, the writer does not believe the agents' reports may be accepted literally.

For one thing, evidence indicates that there were agents, although perhaps they were fairly rare exceptions, who found the combination of allotment and leasing of Indian lands a lucrative business for themselves. For another thing —what was no doubt more generally true—allotment had become established as the official policy and all who were connected with the Indian Service must have been influenced, consciously or unconsciously by that fact. Falling in line with the policy did not necessarily imply sycophancy or opportunism. It would require considerable intellectual independence for an agent to stand out against the policy, whatever he might see about him in the way of its tangible results. He would need great confidence, even audacity, to pit his judgment against the convictions of all the "better minds" of the day. Again, it may be said, the allotment policy began and continued as an act of faith. So it was possible for an agent to report that allotment was working well on his reservation and at the same time submit figures which showed that the greater portion of the Indian lands were leased to white men. Indeed, the testimony which comes even from the friends of the Indian as to the dire results of the leasing policy toward the end of the century makes it seem improbable that the allotment system in the main was working well.

The writer's skepticism as to the real success of the allotment system in the period of the 1890's is based not alone on inference and deduction. The following table contains figures that are pertinent to the question whether or not allotment was producing results.

The figures in the table, while by no means conclusive, indicate that the allotment system was not producing the results which the originators of the policy hoped for. In comparing the number of allotments with the number of families living and working on them, one must bear in mind that several allotments might be made to one family. The act of 1891 which granted eighty acres to every Indian made it possible for one family to possess an even greater number of allotments than before. It is unfortunate that there is no way of knowing the number of specific families allotted and the average number of allotments to each. But the above figures show that the number of families cultivating their allotments was by no means keeping pace with the allotment figures. The number of allotments per family grew from 2.7 in 1890 to 5.4 in 1900. Since it may be supposed that when Indians accepted allotments the family took as many as they could get, and since the only change in the law after 1890 which affected the question of eligibility for allotment was the extension of the privilege to married women, this increasing ration of allotments to families cultivating them suggests a decline of Indian husbandry. Or at least it suggests a failure to reach the goal

## LAND AND CROP STATISTICS

[Unless otherwise indicated the figures are taken from the current volume of the Annual Reports of the Commissioner of Indian Affairs. The figures in parentheses are page references]

| Date | Total number of allotments to date | Total number of leases to date | Number of families living on and cultivating allotments | Number of acres cultivated by Indians | Indian agricultural production (in bushels) | | | | Page |
|---|---|---|---|---|---|---|---|---|---|
| | | | | | Wheat | Oats and barley | Corn | Vegetables | |
| 1890 | 15,166 | | 5,554 | 288,613 | 881,419 | 545,032 | 1,139,297 | 482,500 | (480) |
| 1891 | 17,996 | | 5,883 | | 1,318,218 | 798,001 | 1,830,704 | 541,974 | (106) |
| 1892 | 26,700 | 2 | 7,302 | | 1,825,715 | 875,634 | 1,515,464 | 558,162 | (816) |
| 1893 | 31,261 | 6 | 7,579 | | 1,722,656[1] | 883,170 | 1,373,230 | 462,871 | (723) |
| 1894 | 34,322 | 301 | 8,359 | | 887,809 | 653,631 | 911,655 | 396,133 | (598) |
| 1895 | 39,173 | 631 | 8,366 | 369,974 | 2,016,754[1] | 2,875,349 | 2,226,944[2] | 476,272 | (594) |
| 1896 | 43,587 | 1,564 | 10,045 | | 753,577 | 731,806 | 2,100,316 | 542,538 | (551) |
| 1897 | 46,816 | 2,851 | 10,659 | | 788,192 | 805,466 | 1,123,260 | 703,770 | (510) |
| 1898 | 48,831 | 3,799 | 11,789 | | 664,930 | 599,665 | 1,339,444 | 494,509 | (630) |
| 1899 | 49,842 | 4,984 | 10,704 | | 982,120 | 850,387 | 1,386,977 | 445,935 | (597) |
| 1900 | 58,594 | 7,574 | 10,835 | 343,351 | 935,731 | 722,925 | 1,655,504 | 396,067 | (677) |

1 Over 850,000 bushels of wheat raised by white lessees on Umatilla Reservation.

2 Unspecified amount of wheat, oats, barley, and corn raised by white lessees on Indian lands.

NOTE.—Allotment and leasing totals, 1891–1900 taken from figures given above p. 86.

envisaged by the friends of the Indian. Even more disquieting are the statistics of Indian agriculture. The above
figures show an increase in acreage of Indian farming from
1890 to 1895 which was far from proportionate to the number of allotments made in those years. Then from 1895 to
1900, although more than 19,000 allotments were made,
the area of the land tilled by Indians actually decreased by
over 26,000 acres. Nor if one takes the figures of crop pro-
duction for what they are worth, can one observe the progress in Indian agriculture during these ten years which the
friends of allotment expected.

But it may be argued that it is not fair to judge the allotment system only in terms of agricultural results; that figures on Indian grazing are also pertinent. Yet these figures
themselves reveal no satisfying progress. The figures on the
number of sheep owned by the Indians are of no use because of changes in methods of reporting them. The horse-
and-mule industry showed actual decline from 443,244 in
1890 to 353,387 in 1900. This would not have troubled the
friends of the Indian since they disliked his propensity for
keeping ponies anyway. The cattle industry showed improvement—from 170,419 head in 1890 to 257,610 in
1900.[47] But this progress, again, was hardly commensurate
with the extension of the allotment system. However, these
figures on the Indian cattle herds indicate the soundness of
the agents' recommendations in 1899 that the Indian cattle
industry be expanded.[48] Yet fundamentally, the allotment
theory was an agricultural theory. The thinking of its cre-
ators ran in terms of the Indian as a toiling farmer, living
independently on his tilled acres. There was no equally
strong argument for land in severalty based on a conception of Indian economy as primarily herding. Grazing lands
had been invariably communal lands among the Indians,

where there had been any conception of landed property at all. And the trend of the western cattle industry from open range to vast ranch taught the simple economic lesson, which the least economically minded must have grasped, that the way to develop Indian animal husbandry was not to cut up their lands into eighty-acre or even 160-acre tracts. But above all it was this pastoral life, second only to the chase in encouraging vagrant camp life and heathenism, which the friends of the Indian wanted to smash and replace with the American culture of exalted agrarianism.

The reasons why the Indian allotment policy fell short of the goal which its white sponsors dreamed of are varied, and yet they fit together rather neatly to make a panorama of American life in the 1890's. As the writer has discussed at some length, there was the fundamental fact that allotment with all its cultural implications was alien to the way of Indian life. If the allotment system were to have succeeded, the Indian would, culturally, have had to be made over. The significance of this fact was never fully grasped by the philanthropists and the Government. Individual land ownership was supposed to have some magic in it to transform an Indian hunter into a busy farmer. As for education, it would be enough to inculcate in him the forms if not the substance of the American social heritage. So the Indian, hopefully if not enthusiastically, went, unprepared, out upon his allotment, as an unarmed man would go unwittingly into a forest of wild beasts.

For if white land seekers and the business promoters did not create the allotment system, they at least turned it to their own good use. Where the land was valuable, white interests formed a ring about the Indian reservation; a ring which exerted a relentless pressure in all directions, until the force was felt in Washington itself. This pressure came from

fundamental social forces—from the movement of settlement and enterprise, like a great glacier, moving westward
into new lands. It is not surprising that the Government,
in most cases possessed of good intentions and usually determined to withstand the pressure, yielded here and there.

There is plenty of evidence of this pressure at work. In
1890 the Commissioner disapproved of the Government's
yielding unduly. He wrote: "There is always a clamor for
Indian lands, but there is no such pressing need for more
land for white settlement as to justify undue haste in acquiring it . . . . Nor is it good policy to remove Indian tribes
from one place to another, especially from one State or Territory to another, merely to satisfy the selfish ends or to suit
the convenience of the whites. It creates discontent, destroys
the natural attachment for the soil, disturbs whatever progress in localization and settlement may have been made,
and retards progress in every way."[49] One can but marvel at
the prevailing point of view of a public who would require
such an exposition. But the Board of Indian Commissioners believed there were times when justice for the Indians
and profit for the whites could be combined. Their report
for 1890 noted that through cessions of unallotted lands
the Government had "secured for white settlers 13,000,000
acres, which would otherwise remain waste and unproduc-
tive" while the Indians would "receive funds sufficient to
give them a good start in their new life."[50]

First of all, white interests were concerned with the breaking down of the reservation and were apparently working
tirelessly to this end. The friends of the Indian, as has been
said before, looked to allotment as a means of making secure at least "half a loaf" for the Indian. Professor Painter
believed that even the western whites expected (or feared)

that allotment would accomplish this aim. He told the Mohonk Conference in 1889:

The passage of the severalty bill, which substitutes a personal title evidenced by a patent protected by law for a tribal right of occupancy during the good pleasure of Congress or of the Executive, if the reservation is one by executive order, has awakened the frontiersman to the fact that he must secure such concessions, adjustments, and cessions he desires at once, before allotments are made, since it will be more difficult to set aside the provisions of this law than to procure the abrogation of a treaty made with a people too feeble to enforce it. Hence this great activity and increasing facility in Indian legislation.[51]

A member of the committee for legal assistance that same year urged upon the Mohonk Conference the necessity of hastening allotment among the Mission Indians of California. He said:

The work should not, however, be delayed for any uncertain action of Congress, but meanwhile be pressed under the severalty act; for in southern California, as elsewhere, the local press spends much of its energy in urging the breaking up of the reservations and the removal of the Indians, giving an exaggerated impression of the size and value of the reserves, the number and condition of the Indians, and their injurious effect upon the welfare of the country. Such attacks are supposed to emanate from the whole body of settlers in the vicinity of the different Indian settlements; but, to the close observer, it is evident that, while they influence to some degree the feeling of whole communities, they are chiefly inspired by a few seeking private gain.[52]

143

Apparently the pressure in this particular case was so strong that the friends of the Indian found they had to yield in order to salvage anything for him. An investigating committee reported to the Board of Indian Commissioners early in 1890 that an agreement had been reached with the Potrero Mission Indians which settled a dispute with the Southern Pacific Railway Company. The Indians had objected to Congress's giving some of their lands to the railroad for a right-of-way. The agreement moved the Indians into a valley, gave to the railroad other lands in exchange for those to be occupied by the Indians, and cut down the reservation from 144 to twenty-six sections. The committee said, "A settlement such as is proposed, at first glance would seem to be a great sacrifice to the Indians." The committee went on to show that by the new arrangement the Indians would be secure in water rights and in their holding of the best fruit lands. The committee concluded, "It is also to be kept in mind that it is hopeless to attempt to stem the progress of an active white settlement, even if it is desirable, and a pacific adjustment of disputed titles, such as that proposed, is not to be rated as of little value."[53]

Besides the lands that were thrown open to settlement, white men were interested in tribal lands that remained. This was especially true of the cattlemen. Professor Painter dealt at length with this question in his speech before the 1889 Mohonk Conference. He said, "We need now to face the fact, and deal with it, that the surplus of the reservation, after allotment, is a danger that threatens much. . . ." He explained how the Winnebagoes had leased their surplus lands for grazing, but because of "collusion between the officials in charge and the cattle men, whose interests were looked after by influential politicians," 15,000 cattle were grazed on their lands for $300, when the rent should have been at least $7,500. He added that the $300 went mostly for bribes.[54]

When it came to the actual designation of allotments, white influence was also busy. General Whittlesey, of the Board of Indian Commissioners, said to the Mohonk Conference in 1891, "Another hindrance [to the allotting of lands] is the influence brought to bear by surrounding white settlers, who are waiting to get possession of the lands that may be reserved after allotments are completed. If there are valuable tracts of land, they try to prevent those lands from being allotted, and to prevent Indians from selecting them, by bribery and by other means."[55] Miss Fletcher contributed from the rich store of her allotment experience to a discussion of this point at a Board of Indian Commissioners' conference in 1890. She said:

> The whites say, "You are giving the very best land to the Indians." I hope you will never have a thousandth part of the lectures I have had to take for pursuing this policy. I have had people tell me the capacity and incapacity, the powers and the lack of powers of the Indians and how useless this effort was to benefit them, and that I should be throwing away this fine land. I have had committees follow me around in my allotment work to look after the interests of the white people. I have been talked to in a pleasant manner and in an unpleasant manner on the subject of my pushing the Indians where they are bound to die out, and annoying white people with neighbors they did not want to have.[56]

This sort of activity on the part of the white neighbors continued through the period. In 1898 the agent of the Mission Tule River Reservation in California wrote: ". . . there is such a stubborn resistance on the part of many white people to the Indians occupying the lands set apart for them that the friction between Indian and white neighbors is constant."[57] Small wonder it seems that there should be such constant complaint from officials and friends of the Indian that so many Indians were located on lands unfit for agriculture.

The whites found various opportunities for exploiting the Indians under the allotment system. In 1890, General Whittlesey reported that there was a growing demand for the Government to distribute among the Indians on a per capita basis tribal funds that had been so heavily swelled by sales of surplus lands. He said, "That is their own desire, and the desire of many of those who surround them, who know how soon such money disappears."[58] The Umatilla agent who found agriculture languishing on his reservation in 1894—especially among the full bloods—wrote: "The few mixed bloods who farm their allotments do so with stock, machinery, and provisions furnished by merchants or bankers, who take a mortgage on the crop, afterwards taking all the crop."[59] And there was a long story of flagrant corruption and exploitation in the activities of lumbering companies who manipulated the allotment system to their great profit, on up into the twentieth century.[60]

By the middle of the 1890's the friends of the Indian began to express dismay at the course their humanitarian policy had taken in the hands of persons who were not always humanitarians. In 1888, the Commissioner was confident that the allotment system was such a threat to the vested interests as to evoke their bitter opposition to the plan. He wrote:

Considerable opposition to the allotment policy has been developed from two sources. Those who believe in the wisdom of tribal ownership, and in the policy of continuing the Indian in his aboriginal customs, habits,

146

and independence, oppose it because it will eventually dissolve his tribal relations and cause his absorption into the body politic. On the other hand, those who expected that the severalty act would immediately open to public settlement long-coveted Indian lands, oppose it because they have learned that these expectations will not be realized.[61]

But apparently the white land seekers did not fare so badly under the Indian allotment system. Professor Painter said to the 1894 Mohonk Conference: "Allotments are ordered, not with reference generally to the conditions of the Indian, but to the greed and demands of the white people about the reservation who wish to secure surplus lands. I could, had I time, call attention to reservations where the effect of allotments has been to set back the Indians for twenty years."[62]

The Indian Rights Association in its report of that year maintained that the first and essential safeguard of the allotment had been neglected—namely, that allotment should be applied according to the needs of the Indian. The report maintained that this principle had been "flagrantly disregarded" and went on to say: "Reservations were designated for this purpose [allotment] in many cases by order of the President, and others by means of treaties, procured by means which ought to bring the blush of shame to every citizen, where the greed of the whites, not the interest of the Indians, demanded it. Irreparable injury was thus inflicted upon a number of tribes from which they will slowly, if ever, wholly recover."[63] In 1895 the Commissioner showed himself well aware of the forces that were crippling Indian development. He made a shrewd comment on his times and a significant forecast. He said: "The whites in some sections of the country seem to have very little respect for the rights of Indians who have segregated themselves from their tribes and sought to avail themselves of the benefits of the Indian homestead and allotment laws enacted expressly for them by Congress, and I apprehend that the opposition to them will increase as the public domain grows less and less."[64]

Thus it is clear that the Indian Administration was continuously struggling against terrific odds in its efforts to preserve for the Indian some freedom and opportunity as against the encroachment of white enterprise. And under the constant pressure of many of its powerful citizens the white government made what now appears to be fatal mistakes in administration. One student of the allotment movement believes that the act of 1891 was the most important step toward ruin. This law by granting the Indian the right to lease and at the same time allotting to each member of the family—to babies and octogenarians—an equal amount of land developed in the Indian idleness and avarice. Children ceased to be a responsibility and became indirectly a source of revenue through their leased allotments. As a result the family was disrupted as a producing unit and the Indian's interest became pecuniary instead of industrial.[65] The present writer agrees with this analysis, but he is inclined to think that basically the leasing policy in almost any form would have meant ultimate defeat for the allotment system.

To be sure, if the Government had thrown most of its effort into industrial education and, at the same time, could have held the leasing down only to those cases where it was crystal clear that the allottee was unable to use his land, the allotment system might have survived the leasing practice. But of course the powerful and steady pressure from the whites and from the Indians themselves meant that the leasing policy would swerve with these forces and not be held fast by far-sightedness and restraint. Congress yielded and removed almost every restriction upon the leasing practice. So the Indian came more and more to look upon land as a source of revenue from the labor of someone else. And he was started on this course almost at the outset of what was to be his career as a hard-working, independent farmer. Of course this demoralization by no means reached all Indians. There were unquestionably many instances where the leasing of allotments was a practical and wise solution of an Indian's problem. Nor was leasing applied to the greater number of allotments in this period. It is unfortunate that there are no figures which show the amount of allotted land which was leased by 1900. There are no figures even to show how many allotments were leased, since in some cases one lease might cover the holdings of several Indians.[66] The only figures available are those quoted in the table above, and they show that leasing was developing fast toward the end of the century—that 7,574 leases had been approved by 1900.[67] There is no way of telling what relation this figure bears to that of 58,594 allotments granted by 1900 or to the figure of 10,835 families who were living on and cultivating their allotments in that year. Agents reported at times that Indians lived on their allotments and cultivated portions of them and leased the remainder to whites.[68] From what these figures suggest, it would certainly not be true to say that the leasing policy dominated the allotment system in this period. But the point is that a practice was begun which was carried far in the next century and which retarded Indian agricultural development. Of the 6,463,840 acres agricultural lands allotted to Indians by 1916, 2,357,542 acres were in the hands of lessees.[69]

Furthermore, the leasing of allotments must be regarded

as a step toward their sale. Senator Dawes in 1890 warned the friends of the Indian that if the white man once got his foot upon Indian land he would never take it off.[70] There was much truth in this statement. Especially would it be hard to make the white man get off when the Indian was not anxious to see him go. Accustomed to thinking of his allotment in terms of rent, the Indian landlord could be easily persuaded to seek the right to sell his land for a sum that was immediately greater than the periodic revenue from his leasing. In 1890 Senator Dawes told how various tribes were beseeching the Government to distribute to them their tribal funds. One of the tribes he cited was the Osages. He said: "The Osages, who have in their wealth depreciated and gone back year after year for twenty years, think the wisest way is to take the seven millions or more belonging to them in the treasury, and have a great feast with it as long as it will last."[71] With such prodigal ideas of tribal finance the Indian could hardly be expected to show much providence in his personal affairs. And it was patent that he did not. Yet there were officials in the Indian Service who favored the alienability of Indian lands. As early as 1890, when allotment was just getting under way on a large scale, the secretary of the Wisconsin Indian Association reported that the Oneida agent had recommended to Washington that legislation be passed giving his Indians immediately patents in fee. The Association was up in arms over the matter.[72] In 1898 the Quapaw agent wrote that leasing had been highly successful on his reservation and that he believed the most progressive Indians should be allowed to alienate portions of their lands.[73] Congress in the 1890's began the process of breaking down the safeguard of inalienability which had been thrown around Indian allotments and which was almost completely dissolved by the Burke Act of 1906.[74] In 1893 a law was passed cutting down the trust period for the allottees among the Puyallup Indians from the original twenty-five years to ten. In 1894 Congress authorized the Citizen Potawatomis and Absentee Shawnees in Indian Territory to sell, with the Secretary's approval, all of each allotment in excess of eighty acres. Members of those tribes who lived outside the Territory were to be free to sell what they pleased.[75]

Against these acts the Indian Rights Association protested vigorously, as showing a dangerous trend, and the Board of Indian Commissioners and the Mohonk Conference joined the Association in denouncing the act of 1894.[76] The friends of the Indian sensed that the breach had been made in the dike.

A contemporary writer gave a terse summary of the shortcomings in the development of the allotment policy. In his *The Indians of To-day*, published in 1900, George Bird Grinnell wrote: "The fatally weak points in the allotment law, as now carried out, lie in the tendency to apply it to all tribes, no matter what their condition, progress or situation, in the provision that citizenship shall go with allotments and in subsequent legislation allowing allottees to lease, or in some cases even to sell, their lands. In all these respects the policy is radically wrong and should be changed."[77]

Although these acts of the Government today seem serious mistakes, there are many things which the fairminded critic must consider and which must temper his judgment of the case. In the first place, one who reads the records must conclude that in the main the acts of the Government were in good faith. They were for the most part sincere efforts to defend and help the Indian. In the second place, the Government in its Indian policies had to deal with the dominating elements of the American economic order. At almost every point the Government had to contend with the economic interests not only of expanding corporate wealth but of millions of settlers—ordinary people, citizens of the democracy, voters. From the first, the Government was doomed to lose the fight. Indeed, in the matter of Indian policy especially, one cannot indict the Government without indicting a people. In the third place, it must be remembered that the theories behind the Indian policies were logical elements of the prevailing social philosophy. It was not merely the case that the Government was forced by the pressure of private interests into wholesale allotment, leasing, and the removal of restrictions on alienation. All of these proposals harmonized with the laissez-faire theory which produced allotment.

It must be remembered that allotment was not originally conceived as an educational technique which would require great effort and care in administration. The Government was not to run a colossal nursery school. Allotment was to work all by itself. Through allotment the magical principle of private property was to teach, develop, and refine the Indians as it had supposedly done everyone else. If the Indian was taught acquisitiveness and property put within his reach, then all would go well. This remained the dominating idea of the friends of the Indian. In 1896 President Gates of Amherst College addressed the Mohonk Conference as its presiding officer in words which show the perdurance of the American faith in self-interest. He said:

We have, to begin with, the absolute need of awakening in the savage Indian broader desires and ampler wants. To bring him out of savagery into citizenship we must make the Indian more intelligently selfish before we can make him unselfishly intelligent. We need to *awaken in him wants.* In his dull savagery he must be touched by the wings of the divine angel of discontent. Then he begins to look forward, to reach out. The desire for property of his own may become an intense educating force. The wish for a home of his own awakens him to new efforts. Discontent with the tepee and the starving rations of the Indian camp in winter is needed to get the Indian out of the blanket and into trousers,—and trousers with a pocket in them, and with *a pocket that aches to be filled with dollars!* . . . The truth is, that there can be no strongly developed personality without the teaching of property, —material property, and property in thoughts and convictions that are one's own. By acquiring property, man puts forth his personality and lays hold of matter by his own thought and will. Property has been defined as "objectified will." We all go to school to property, if we use it wisely. No one has the right to the luxury of giving away, until he has learned the luxury of earning and possessing. The Saviour's teaching is full of illustrations of the right use of property. I imagine that we shall look back from that larger life which lies before us "on the farther side of the river of death," and shall regard the property we have held and used here, not as in itself an object and an end, but much as those of us who have had the benefit of kindergarten training look back now upon the little prizes and gifts that were put into our hands in the kindergarten classes, things which were of no sort of value or consequence except as out of their use we got training for the larger life, and for the right use of stronger powers.

There is an immense moral training that comes from the use of property. And the Indian has had all that to learn . . . .[78]

Such a transcendental notion of property as a guiding principle in life would not lead to a theory which required the Government to undertake the active training of the Indians. Indeed, "strong government," and "paternalism," in Indian affairs had in the past been identified with oppression. The friends of the Indian turned away from all this as their forefathers had turned away from Great Britain. And for Americans the new direction was toward laissez-faire and freedom. The Government was to *protect* the Indians; but, as Lyman Abbott said in 1887, the Indian (it was hoped) would not be cared for by the executive branch of the Government: like everyone else he was to come under the protection of the courts.[79] The friends of the Indian, therefore, would not be urging new functions upon an organ of the Government which they had already declared to be moribund. In specific situations, however, the philanthropists felt the need of Government action. In 1899 the Board of Indian Commissioners recommended that there be set up in the service an effective registry of Indian births, marriages, and deaths. But characteristically the Board hastened to add (with its own italics), " . . . our Board is *recommending additional machinery* in the Indian service, *only in order to hasten the period at which all special laws for, and all special administration of Indian affairs, may come to an end.*"[80]

It is only fair to give a contemporary his chance to summarize and justify the Indian policy in the nineteenth century. The Reverend J. M. Buckley, D. D., editor of the *Christian Advocate*, said to the Mohonk Conference in 1889: "I do not believe that our fathers committed an unpardonable sin when they assumed that the Indians did not own this whole continent . . . . I therefore do not feel that those who discovered this country, and found it inhabited by savages, and took possession of it to introduce civilization, committed the unpardonable sin. They did what the world had been doing from the beginning of history till then, and what it has been doing ever since . . . ."[81]

But, of course, the policy of the people who came here was a compound of greed and hatred, necessity and conscience; and from the beginning till now all these elements have been at work, sometimes one in the ascendancy, sometimes another.

# NOTES

Uniform titles have been used for various series of documents cited in the notes, even though the exact titles might have varied in some cases. The year is indicated after the title. The annual reports of the Commissioner of Indian Affairs are cited in their separately published form; they are also to be found in the annual reports of the Secretary of the Interior in the serial set of Congressional documents. Material from the Lake Mohonk Conferences is cited from the separately published *Proceedings* of the Conferences; the same material is printed in the annual reports of the Board of Indian Commissioners.

## I. THE GENERAL ALLOTMENT LAW (DAWES ACT)

1. "Allotment of Lands in Severalty among Indian Tribes: Memorial of the Creek Nation on the Subject of Lands in Severalty among the Several Indian Tribes, with Accompanying Papers," *House Miscellaneous Document* No. 18, 47 Congress, 2 session, serial 2115, p. 36.
2. Charles J. Kappler, ed., *Indian Affairs: Laws and Treaties* (2 vols., Washington, 1904), II, 87–88; *Report of the Commissioner of Indian Affairs*, 1885, pp. 320–21; *ibid.*, 1891, p. 40.
3. *United States Statutes at Large*, V, 349–51.

4. *Report of the Commissioner of Indian Affairs*, 1885, pp. 320–21.

5. "Lands in Severalty to Indians," *House Report* No. 1576, 46 Congress, 2 session, serial 1938, p. 7.

6. *United States Statutes at Large*, XVIII, 420.

7. *Report of the Commissioner of Indian Affairs*, 1870, p. 9; *ibid.*, 1871, p. 5.

8. See *House Miscellaneous Document* No. 18, 47 Congress, 2 session, serial 2115, p. 26; *Report of the Commissioner of Indian Affairs*, 1872, pp. 82–105.

9. *Ibid.*, 1873, p. 4.

10. *Ibid.*, 1876, p. ix.

11. Report of the Secretary of the Interior, 1874, *House Executive Document* No. 1, part 5, 43 Congress, 2 session, serial 1639, pp. v–vii; Report of the Secretary of the Interior, 1875, *House Executive Document* No. 1, part 5, 44 Congress, 1 session, serial 1680, p. v.

12. Report of the Secretary of the Interior, 1876, *House Executive Document* No. 1, part 5, 44 Congress, 2 session, serial 1749, p. v.

13. Report of the Secretary of the Interior, 1877, *House Executive Document* No. 1, part 5, 45 Congress, 2 session, serial 1800, p. xi.

14. *Report of the Commissioner of Indian Affairs*, 1876, p. ix.

15. Report of the Secretary of the Interior, 1879, *House Executive Document* No. 1, part 5, 46 Congress, 2 session, serial 1910, p. 12.

16. *Report of the Commissioner of Indian Affairs*, 1883, p. 160.

17. *Ibid.*, 1886, p. xx.

18. *Ibid.*, 1880, p. xvii.

19. "Report of the Joint Committee Appointed to Consider the Expediency of Transferring the Indian Bureau to the War Department," *House Report* No. 93, 45 Congress, 3 session, serial 1866, pp. 3–20.

20. *Congressional Record*, VIII, 864 (January 31, 1879). See also *House Report* No. 165, 45 Congress, 3 session, serial 1866.

21. *Congressional Record*, X, 274 (January 12, 1880); X, 1394 (March 8, 1880); X, 3507 (May 19, 1880).

22. *House Report* No. 1576, 46 Congress, 2 session, serial 1938.

23. *Congressional Record*, X, 3507 (May 19, 1880).

24. *Lake Mohonk Conference Proceedings*, 1885, p. 38.

25. *Congressional Record*, XI, 778–79 (January 20, 1881). For debate on the question of amending the bill to extend citizenship to the Indian, see *ibid.*, XI, 875–82 (January 24, 1881).

26. *Report of the Commissioner of Indian Affairs*, 1884, p. xiii; *ibid.*, 1885, p. xv; "Allowance of Lands in Severalty to Indians," *House Report* No. 2247, 48 Congress, 2 session, serial 2328.

27. *United States Statutes at Large,* XXII, 42, 341–43; XXIII, 340–41.

28. George F. Parker, ed., *The Writings and Speeches of Grover Cleveland* (New York, 1892), pp. 410–15.

29. Report of Lieutenant General P. H. Sheridan, October 10, 1886, in *Report of the Secretary of War,* 1886, pp. 76–78.

30. *United States Statutes at Large,* XXIV, 388–90. The writer regrets that time has not permitted a careful study of the Government documents, especially of the *Congressional Record,* relating to the Dawes bill. Such a study might by implication throw some light on the forces at work to secure its passage. There is a well-founded suspicion that all the motives of the legislators were not concerned merely with the Indian's welfare. The study would at least show the drift of opinion. In 1887 President Amelia S. Quinton told the Women's National Indian Association that passage of the Dawes bill eight years previously would have been "an absolute impossibility." She said that the women's petition with 100,000 signatures, which was presented to Congress in 1882, met with "dense ignorance," "prejudice," and the influence of the "Indian Ring." *Address of the President of the Women's National Indian Association on Current Indian Legislation, Work Needed, Etc.* (Philadelphia, 1887), pp. 7–8. In its last stages the bill met with no opposition at all. Debate dealt only with details.

31. Certain tribes were exempted from the provisions of the act, viz., the Five Civilized Tribes, the Osages, Miamis and Peorias, Sacs and Foxes, in Indian Territory, the Senecas in New York State, and the inhabitants of the strip south of the Sioux in Nebraska (Section 8).

## II. AIMS AND MOTIVES OF THE ALLOTMENT MOVEMENT

1. *Congressional Record,* XVIII, 191 (December 15, 1886).

2. *Lake Mohonk Conference Proceedings,* 1885, p. 37.

3. *Report of the Commissioner of Indian Affairs,* 1877, pp. 75–76. See also *ibid.,* 1879, p. 25; *ibid.,* 1885, p. 21; *ibid.,* 1886, pp. vii–x.

4. *Ibid.,* 1882, p. 86. See also *ibid.,* 1878, p. 48; *ibid.,* 1877, p. 121; *ibid.,* 1876, pp. 58–59.

5. *Ibid.,* 1873, p. 4. See also *ibid.,* 1877, p. 51.

6. *Lake Mohonk Conference Proceedings,* 1885, p. 56. J. H. Oberly was Commissioner in 1888 and until March, 1889, when General T. J. Morgan was appointed.

7. *Congressional Record,* XI, 906 (January 25, 1881).

8. *Lake Mohonk Conference Proceedings,* 1885, p. 43. See also letter of the Commissioner to Secretary Schurz, January 27, 1879, in *House Report* No. 165, 45 Congress, 3 session, serial 1866, p. 2.

9. Memorial to Congress from Cherokee Nation in *Congressional Record*, XI, 781 (January 20, 1881).

10. *House Report* No. 1576, 46 Congress, 2 session, serial 1938, p. 10.

11. *Lake Mohonk Conference Proceedings*, 1889, p. 96.

12. Alice C. Fletcher and Francis LaFlesche, *The Omaha Tribe* (Twenty-seventh Annual Report of the Bureau of American Ethnology, Washington, 1911), pp. 273–75.

13. *Report of the Commissioner of Indian Affairs*, 1864, p. 332.

14. *Congressional Record*, XI, 781 (January 20, 1881). See also *House Report* No. 1576, 46 Congress, 2 session, serial 1938, pp. 7–10.

15. *Congressional Record*, XI, 785 (January 20, 1881).

16. *Ibid.*, 783 (January 20, 1881).

17. *House Report* No. 1576, 46 Congress, 2 session, serial 1938, p. 8.

18. Frederic Bancroft, ed., *The Speeches, Correspondence, and Political Papers of Carl Schurz* (6 vols., New York, 1913), IV, 143.

19. *Lake Mohonk Conference Proceedings*, 1884, p. 8. See also letter from the Commissioner to the Secretary of the Interior, January 27, 1879, in *House Report* No. 165, 45 Congress, 3 session, serial 1866, p. 2.

20. Fletcher and LaFlesche, *The Omaha Tribe*, pp. 635–36; "Memorial of the Members of the Omaha Tribe of Indians, for a Grant of Land in Severalty," *Senate Miscellaneous Document* No. 31, 47 Congress, 1 session, serial 1993.

21. *Lake Mohonk Conference Proceedings*, 1887, p. 68.

22. Bancroft, *Papers of Carl Schurz*, IV, 142.

23. *Ibid.*, 141, 146; *Lake Mohonk Conference Proceedings*, 1889, pp. 9–10.

24. Bancroft, *Papers of Carl Schurz*, IV, 126.

25. Address of Walter Allen, *Lake Mohonk Conference Proceedings*, 1886, p. 41. See also *ibid.*, 1885, p. 53.

26. Commissioner to Secretary Schurz, January 27, 1879, in *House Report* No. 165, 45 Congress, 3 session, serial 1866, p. 3. See also *Report of the Commissioner of Indian Affairs*, 1881, p. xxiii.

27. *Congressional Record*, XVIII, 190 (December 15, 1886).

28. Report of the Secretary of the Interior, 1880, *House Executive Document* No. 1, part 5, 46 Congress, 3 session, serial 1959, p. 12.

29. *Report of the Commissioner of Indian Affairs*, 1885, p. 88. At the same time one often encounters remarks like the following from the report of an agent: ". . . profane language is never heard, unless among those who have learned the white man's way." *Ibid.*, 1880, p. xliv.

30. *Ibid.*, p. xvii.

31. *Congressional Record*, XI, 934 (January 26, 1881).

32. *Ibid.*, 783 (January 20, 1881).

33. *Ibid.*, XVII, 1559 (February 17, 1886). Senator Morgan in 1881 had charged that the Government had not dared to allot lands to the Indians of Indian Territory, because it was a known fact that white settlers were hanging about the lands waiting for them to be opened up by allotment. *Ibid.*, XI, 786 (January 20, 1881). On the other hand Judge Draper of New York, told the fifth Lake Mohonk Conference that white citizens near the reservations in his State were opposed to allotting lands to the Indians for fear they would quickly dissipate them and become public charges. *Lake Mohonk Conference Proceedings*, 1887, pp. 18–19.

34. *Congressional Record*, XI, 783 (January 20, 1881).

35. *House Report* No. 1576, 46 Congress, 2 session, serial 1938, p. 10.

36. Frederic L. Paxson, *History of the American Frontier, 1763–1893* (Boston, 1924), Chapter LVII.

37. Samuel Taylor, "The Origins of the Dawes Act of 1887" (Philip Washburn Prize thesis, Harvard College, 1927), pp. 25–42.

38. *Ibid.*, pp. 26–28.

39. *Ibid.*, p. 59. The author significantly points out that the only concerted opposition of western senators to the Coke bill was directed against the proposal to extend citizenship, and therefore legal protection, to the Indians. *Ibid.*, pp. 50–56.

40. *Ibid.*, p. 45.

41. Conference of the Board of Indian Commissioners with Missionary Boards and Indian Rights Associations, January 6, 1887, *Report of the Board of Indian Commissioners*, 1886, p. 123. See also Taylor, "Origins of the Dawes Act," p. 64.

42. *Lake Mohonk Conference Proceedings*, 1889, pp. 78–81.

43. Paxson, *American Frontier*, p. 548.

44. *Ibid.*, pp. 323–512, *passim.*

45. *Report of the Commissioner of Indian Affairs*, 1883, p. 33. The Flathead agent wrote the same year, "As a proof that the Indians of this reservation, while undoubtedly brave, are also law-abiding, I refer with pride to the fact of the completion of the Northern Pacific Railroad through their lands, and against their strongest wishes, without any annoyance or opposition being offered to the railroad company that for a moment could be termed serious." *Ibid.*, p. 101.

46. *Report of the Commissioner of Indian Affairs*, 1887, pp. 272–85.

47. *Ibid.*, p. xxxviii.

48. *Ibid.*, 1885, p. xxxiii.

49. *Ibid.*, 1888, pp. 290–344.

50. *Ibid.*, 1889, pp. 425–62.

51. *United States Statutes at Large,* XXIV, 391.

52. *Report of the Commissioner of Indian Affairs,* 1898, pp. 407–57. See *ibid.* for intervening years under "legislation."

53. Joseph Gilpin Pyle, *The Life of James J. Hill* ( 2 vols., Garden City, New York, 1917), I, 384.

54. *Ibid.,* I, 386; *United States Statutes at Large,* XXIV, 402; XXV, 113.

55. Pyle, *James J. Hill,* I, 385–86.

56. Parker, *Writings of Cleveland,* p. 97. See also *Report of the Commissioner of Indian Affairs,* 1888, pp. 290–344.

57. Robert M. LaFollette, *LaFollette's Autobiography: A Personal Narrative of Political Experiences* (Madison, Wisconsin, 1913), pp. 71–75.

58. *Report of the Commissioner of Indian Affairs,* 1886, p. 243.

59. *United States Statutes at Large,* XXII, 328.

60. Report of the Secretary of the Interior, 1883, *House Executive Document No.* 1, part 5, 48 Congress, 1 session, serial 2190, pp. xvii–xviii; *Lake Mohonk Conference Proceedings,* 1883, pp. 4–5.

61. *Ibid.,* pp. 5–8.

62. *Ibid.,* p. 5.

63. *Ibid.,* 1885, p. 52.

64. *Report of the Commissioner of Indian Affairs,* 1887, p. 144.

65. *Report of the Indian Rights Association,* 1887, pp. 36, 38.

## III. ORGANIZATIONS SUPPORTING ALLOTMENT

1. Laurence F. Schmeckebier, *The Office of Indian Affairs: Its History, Activities, and Organization* (Baltimore, 1927), pp. 57, 292.

2. *Report of the Board of Indian Commissioners,* 1876, p. 10.

3. *Lake Mohonk Conference Proceedings,* 1885, pp. 46–47.

4. Constitution of Women's National Indian Association, Article II, in *Fourth Annual Report of the Women's National Indian Association,* 1884, p. 57.

5. *Address of the President of the Women's National Indian Association on Current Indian Legislation, Work Needed, Etc.* (Philadelphia, 1887).

6. *Lake Mohonk Conference Proceedings,* 1885, pp. 46–47.

7. *Ibid.*

8. *Fourth Annual Report of the Women's National Indian Association,* 1884, p. 12.

9. *Ibid.,* pp. 49–50.

10. *Address of the President of the Women's National Indian Association,* 1887, p. 8.

11. *Fourth Annual Report of the Women's National Indian Association*, 1884, p. 16. General Whittlesey, secretary of the Board of Indian Commissioners in 1890 mentioned the women as being especially responsible for the allotment policy. *Lake Mohonk Conference Proceedings*, 1890, p. 12.

12. *Report of the Indian Rights Association*, 1883, pp. 5, 6.

13. *Ibid.*, 1886, p. 6.

14. *Ibid.*, 1884, pp. 7–8; *ibid.*, 1886, pp. 4, 11–14.

15. *Ibid.*, 1886, pp. 3–4.

16. *Ibid.*, 1887, p. 67.

17. *Ibid.*, 1886, inside front cover. It is interesting that Senator Dawes had been a prohibition worker. See *Report of the Board of Indian Commissioners*, 1886, p. 130.

18. *Report of the Indian Rights Association*, 1887, p. 36.

19. *Ibid.*, p. 14.

20. *Lake Mohonk Conference Proceedings*, 1887, p. 70.

21. *Ibid.*, 1885, p. 1. [The annual Conference at Lake Mohonk, near New Paltz, New York, became the principal forum for the discussion of Indian policy. The members, who attended for three days each autumn as guests of Albert K. Smiley, heard formal papers on Indian matters, discussed the topics presented, and formulated recommendations. The Conference had no legal status, other than as a loose extension of the Board of Indian Commissioners. Its work was to marshal public sentiment behind specific measures and to propagandize these measures in the press and in the halls of government. Through its annual reports, issued under the title *Proceedings of the Lake Mohonk Conference of Friends of the Indian,* through coverage of its activities and recommendations in the press, and through close cooperation with such groups as the Women's National Indian Association and the Indian Rights Association, it in fact became what its promoters intended—a dominant force in the formulation of Indian policy. The Conference met each year from 1883 to 1916; by the turn of the century, when it considered its Indian work largely accomplished, the Conference added concern for the inhabitants of the overseas possessions acquired by the United States and described itself as "Friends of the Indian and Other Dependent Peoples." Editor's note.]

22. *Ibid.*, 1883, pp. 8–9.

23. *Report of the Indian Rights Association*, 1887, p. 36.

24. Quoted by Lawrence Lindley, associate secretary of the Indian Rights Association, in an unpublished manuscript. This is an excellent brief summary of the whole allotment policy and has been of great use to the present writer.

25. *Preamble, Platform, and Constitution of the National Indian Defence Association* (Washington, 1885), p. 5.
26. *Ibid.*, p. 6.
27. *Ibid.*, p. 5.
28. The Reverend Dorsey was also a member of the Anthropological Society of Washington in 1888. Samuel Taylor, "The Origins of the Dawes Act of 1887" (Philip Washburn Prize thesis, Harvard College, 1927), pp. 60–61, calls the members of the Association "high-minded but utterly impractical" and says they were led by a professional reformer. [There is a brief account of the National Indian Defence Association in Loring B. Priest, *Uncle Sam's Stepchildren: The Reformation of United States Indian Policy, 1865–1887* (New Brunswick, New Jersey, 1942), p. 86. Editor's note.]
29. See above, pp. 9–10.
30. Alice C. Fletcher and Francis LaFlesche, *The Omaha Tribe* (Twenty-seventh Annual Report of the Bureau of American Ethnology, Washington, 1911).
31. *Congressional Record*, XI, 911 (January 25, 1881).
32. *Report of the Indian Rights Association*, 1887, p. 36.

## IV.  INDIAN ATTITUDES AND CAPACITIES

1. *Congressional Record*, XI, 787 (January 20, 1881).
2. See agents' reports in *Report of the Commissioner of Indian Affairs*, 1876, *passim; ibid.*, 1878, p. 142; *ibid.*, 1880, pp. 25, 50, 87, 171; *ibid.*, 1881, pp. 22, 25, 132, 177; *ibid.*, 1882, *passim;* and *ibid,* 1883, *passim.*
3. *House Report* No. 1319, 46 Congress, 2 session, serial 1937.
4. "Memorial of the Members of the Omaha Tribe of Indians, for a Grant of Land in Severalty," *Senate Miscellaneous Document* No. 31, 47 Congress, 1 session, serial 1993.
5. *Report of the Commissioner of Indian Affairs*, 1886, p. 247.
6. *Ibid.*, 1876, p. 124. See also *ibid.*, 1880, p. 25.
7. Alice C. Fletcher and Francis LaFlesche, *The Omaha Tribe* (Twenty-seventh Annual Report of the Bureau of American Ethnology, Washington, 1911), p. 637; *Report of the Commissioner of Indian Affairs*, 1882, p. 112.
8. *House Report* No. 1576, 46 Congress, 2 session, serial 1938, p. 7.
9. "Seneca Nation of New York Indians," *House Executive Document* No. 83, 47 Congress, 1 session, serial 2027; "Allotment of Lands in Severalty among Indian Tribes: Memorial of the Creek Nation," *House Miscellaneous Document* No. 18, 47 Congress, 2 session, serial 2115.

10. *Ibid.*, p. 26.

11. *Report of the Commissioner of Indian Affairs*, 1883, p. 85. See also, *ibid.*, 1886, pp. 98–99.

12. *Lake Mohonk Conference Proceedings*, 1884, p. 26.

13. *Congressional Record*, XI, 781 (January 20, 1881).

14. *Lake Mohonk Conference Proceedings*, 1885, pp. 43–44.

15. *Report of the Commissioner of Indian Affairs*, 1884, p. 94.

16. *House Executive Document* No. 83, 47 Congress, 1 session, serial 2027, p. 2.

17. Samuel Taylor, "The Origins of the Dawes Act of 1887" (Philip Washburn Prize thesis, Harvard College, 1927), pp. 26–27, 60–61.

18. *Report of the Commissioner of Indian Affairs*, 1886, p. vi.

19. *Ibid.*, p. 155.

20. *Congressional Record*, XI, 780 (January 20, 1881).

21. See letter of the Director of the Smithsonian Institution, *ibid.*, XI, 911 (January 26, 1881); *Report of the Commissioner of Indian Affairs*, 1883, p. 53; *ibid.*, 1887, pp. 88, 112.

22. *Ibid.*, 1885, p. 44.

23. Comments of Miss Fletcher, *Lake Mohonk Conference Proceedings*, 1884, p. 26.

24. *Senate Report* No. 243, 47 Congress, 1 session, serial 2004, p. 1.

25. *Report of the Commissioner of Indian Affairs*, 1885, pp. lxxi–lxxii, 169–70.

26. *Congressional Record*, XI, 783 (January 20, 1881).

27. *Report of the Commissioner of Indian Affairs*, 1880, p. xl.

28. *Ibid.*, 1881, p. xxiv.

29. *Ibid.*, p. 171.

30. *Ibid.*, 1885, p. 114.

31. *Ibid.*, 1886, pp. 69–70.

32. *Ibid.*, 1880, p. xxxiv.

33. *Senate Miscellaneous Document* No. 31, 47 Congress, 1 session, serial 1993, p. 8. See also Fletcher and LaFlesche, *The Omaha Tribe*, pp. 247–48, 636–39. For accounts of how other Indians were successfully learning the white man's way, see *Report of the Commissioner of Indian Affairs*, 1876, p. 114; *ibid.*, 1880, p. 137; *ibid.*, 1881, p. xxiii; Mrs. J. B. Dickinson, *Address of the President at the Annual Meeting of the Women's National Indian Association, Philadelphia, Pa., November 17, 1885*, pp. 10–11; *Lake Mohonk Conference Proceedings*, 1884, p. 25; *House Report* No. 1576, 46 Congress, 2 session, serial 1938, pp. 3–5.

34. *Report of the Commissioner of Indian Affairs*, 1876, p. 97.

35. *Ibid.*, 1884, pp. L, 118.

36. *Ibid.*, p. xlix; *Lake Mohonk Conference Proceedings*, 1884, pp.

5–6. See also *Report of the Commissioner of Indian Affairs*, 1885, p. 135.

37. *Ibid.*, 1886, pp. 186–87.

38. *Ibid.*, p. xx.

39. *Ibid.*, pp. 186–87.

40. A member of the Board of Indian Commissioners visited the Omahas in 1887. While he noted much demoralization, he believed the Omahas were in a transitional stage and were making progress. *Report of the Board of Indian Commissioners*, 1887, p. 25.

41. *House Miscellaneous Document* No. 18, 47 Congress, 2 session, serial 2115, p. 18.

42. *Report of the Commissioner of Indian Affairs*, 1878, p. 75.

43. *Ibid.*, p. ix.

44. Report of William H. Waldby, in *Report of the Board of Indian Commissioners*, 1886, p. 13.

45. *Congressional Record*, XI, 781 (January 20, 1881).

46. *House Report* No. 1576, 46 Congress, 2 session, serial 1938, p. 8.

47. *Congressional Record*, XI, 781 (January 20, 1881).

48. *House Miscellaneous Document* No. 18, 47 Congress, 2 session, serial 2115, p. 58.

49. *Report of the Commissioner of Indian Affairs*, 1876, p. 96. The Kickapoo agent wrote in 1877 that several allottees on the reservation had applied to return to common holdings and that others had abandoned the idea of citizenship. *Ibid.*, 1877, p. 119.

50. *Ibid.*, 1885, p. 30.

51. *Ibid.*, p. 133.

52. *Ibid.*, 1884, p. 49.

53. *Ibid.*, 1886, pp. xx–xxi.

54. *House Report* No. 1576, 46 Congress, 2 session, serial 1938, p. 5.

55. Fletcher and LaFlesche, *The Omaha Tribe*, pp. 269, 362–63; Frederick Webb Hodge, ed., *Handbook of American Indians North of Mexico* (Bureau of American Ethnology, Bulletin 30, 2 vols., Washington, 1907–1910), I, 756.

56. *Ibid.*, 24–27.

57. Flora Warren Seymour, "Our Indian Land Policy," *Journal of Land & Public Utility Economics*, II (January, 1926), 93–94. See also Flora Warren Seymour, *The Story of the Red Man* (New York, 1929), p. 366.

58. *Report of the Commissioner of Indian Affairs*, 1886, p. 135. See also *ibid.*, 1887, p. 58.

59. *House Report* No. 1576, 46 Congress, 2 session, serial 1938, pp. 8–9.

60. *Report of the Commissioner of Indian Affairs*, 1887, pp. 56–57,

60. For an analysis of the Indian customs of making gifts and their place in Indian economy, see Margaret Mead, *The Changing Culture of an Indian Tribe* (New York, 1932), pp. 41–46.

61. *House Report* No. 165, 45 Congress, 3 session, serial 1866, p. 2.

## V. THE APPROACH TO THE NEW POLICY

1. *Lake Mohonk Conference Proceedings*, 1887, p. 104.

2. George F. Parker, ed., *The Writings and Speeches of Grover Cleveland* (New York, 1892), p. 420.

3. *Lake Mohonk Conference Proceedings*, 1887, p. 9.

4. *Ibid.*, p. 12.

5. *Ibid.*, p. 9.

6. *Ibid.*, p. 68.

7. *Congressional Record*, XI, 780, 784–85 (January 20, 1881); *House Report* No. 1576, 46 Congress, 2 session, serial 1938, pp. 7–8.

8. *Lake Mohonk Conference Proceedings*, 1885, p. 44.

9. *Report of the Indian Rights Association*, 1886, p. 9.

10. *Report of the Board of Indian Commissioners*, 1887, pp. 6–7. See also *Report of the Indian Rights Association*, 1887, p. 4.

11. *Report of the Commissioner of Indian Affairs*, 1887, pp. vi–vii.

12. *Lake Mohonk Conference Proceedings*, 1887, p. 67.

13. *Report of the Board of Indian Commissioners*, 1887, p. 7; *Report of the Commissioner of Indian Affairs*, 1887, p. vii.

14. *Lake Mohonk Conference Proceedings*, 1887, pp. 63–64, 71–72, 87–88.

15. *Ibid.*, p. 104.

16. *Ibid.*, pp. 60–61.

17. *Ibid.*, p. 32.

18. *Ibid.*, p. 22.

19. *Ibid.*, 1885, p. 39.

20. *Ibid.*, 1887, pp. 3–7, 13–17.

21. *Ibid.*, p. 31.

22. *Ibid.*, pp. 104–106.

23. *Report of the Commissioner of Indian Affairs*, 1887, p. xiv.

24. *Ibid.*, p. xxi.

## VI. THE DEVELOPMENT OF AN EDUCATIONAL POLICY

1. *Report of the Board of Indian Commissioners*, 1887, p. 7; *Lake Mohonk Conference Proceedings*, 1888, pp. 5–41, 72–106.

2. *Report of the Commissioner of Indian Affairs*, 1888, p. xix.

3. *Lake Mohonk Conference Proceedings,* 1884, p. 25.

4. *Ibid.,* 1891, p. 67.

5. *Report of the Board of Indian Commissioners,* 1891, p. 151.

6. *Ibid.,* 1889, p. 152.

7. *Ibid.*

8. George F. Parker, ed., *The Writings and Speeches of Grover Cleveland* (New York, 1892), p. 420.

9. *Lake Mohonk Conference Proceedings,* 1889, pp. 46, 49.

10. *Report of the Board of Indian Commissioners,* 1889, p. 145.

11. *Ibid.,* p. 149.

12. *Lake Mohonk Conference Proceedings,* 1889, p. 39.

13. *Report of the Board of Indian Commissioners,* 1890, pp. 169–72.

14. *Ibid.,* 1889, pp. 149–50.

15. *Lake Mohonk Conference Proceedings,* 1889, p. 15.

16. *Ibid.,* 1894, p. 86.

17. *Ibid.,* 1890, p. 9.

18. *Ibid.,* p. 93. See also his remarks, *ibid.,* 1889, p. 95, and *ibid.,* 1891, p. 68.

19. *Report of the Board of Indian Commissioners,* 1889, p. 148.

20. *Lake Mohonk Conference Proceedings,* 1890, p. 83. See also his remarks to the 1892 Board of Indian Commissioners' conference in *Report of the Board of Indian Commissioners,* 1891, pp. 150–51.

21. See *Lake Mohonk Conference Proceedings,* 1889, pp. 107–11; *Report of the Commissioner of Indian Affairs,* 1892, p. 138.

22. *Lake Mohonk Conference Proceedings,* 1889, p. 62.

23. *Ibid.,* 1890, pp. 80–81. [Much of the opposition to the confirmation of Morgan's appointment came from Roman Catholics, who feared Morgan's hostility to the contract school system, in which Catholic Indian schools were predominant. For details on the controversy, see Harry J. Sievers, "The Catholic Indian School Issue and the Presidential Election of 1892," *Catholic Historical Review,* XXXVIII (July, 1952), 129–55. Editor's note.]

24. *Report of the Commissioner of Indian Affairs,* 1891, p. 53.

25. *Ibid.,* 1889, pp. 94–96.

26. *Ibid.,* pp. 94, 95.

27. *Ibid.,* pp. 99, 101.

28. *Ibid.,* pp. 95, 98.

29. *Ibid.,* pp. 101–102.

30. *Report of the Board of Indian Commissioners,* 1888, pp. 4–5. A missionary told the 1889 Mohonk Conference that on his travels through the reservations he had met nearly all the Indian agents and they unanimously favored compulsory education. *Lake Mohonk Conference Proceedings,* 1889, p. 43.

31. *Ibid.*, pp. 16–34.

32. *Report of the Commissioner of Indian Affairs*, 1890, p. viii. These persons and organizations were the United States Commissioner of Education, the ex-Commissioner, the National Education Association, the American Institute of Instruction, the New York State Teachers' Association, and the various organizations of the friends of the Indian.

33. See Laurence F. Schmeckebier, *The Office of Indian Affairs: Its History, Activities, and Organization* (Baltimore, 1927), p. 223.

34. *Lake Mohonk Conference Proceedings*, 1891, p. 112; *ibid.*, 1893, p. 142.

35. *Report of the Commissioner of Indian Affairs*, 1889, p. 94.

36. *Ibid.*, 1901, p. 39.

37. *Report of the Board of Indian Commissioners*, 1889, p. 148.

38. *Lake Mohonk Conference Proceedings*, 1890, p. 84.

39. *Report of the Commissioner of Indian Affairs*, 1891, p. 40.

40. *Ibid.*, 1889, pp. 11–12.

41. Schmeckebier, *Office of Indian Affairs*, p. 248.

42. *United States Statutes at Large*, XXIII, 92; XXIV, 43; XXV, 233; XXVI, 355, 1008; XXIX, 324.

43. *Report of the Commissioner of Indian Affairs*, 1890, pp. 58–59, 106, 142.

44. *Lake Mohonk Conference Proceedings*, 1891, p. 68.

45. *Report of the Board of Indian Commissioners*, 1897, p. 11.

46. Statistics compiled by Miss Gwen Williams in Employees Section of the Indian Office.

47. *Report of the Commissioner of Indian Affairs*, 1900, p. 656.

48. *Ibid.*, p. 677.

49. *Ibid.*, 1890, p. 59. See also *ibid.*, p. 142.

50. Schmeckebier, *Office of Indian Affairs*, p. 248.

51. *Report of the Commissioner of Indian Affairs*, 1890, p. cxli.

52. *Report of the Board of Indian Commissioners*, 1891, p. 150.

53. *Report of the Commissioner of Indian Affairs*, 1895, p. 151.

54. Quoted in Schmeckebier, *Office of Indian Affairs*, pp. 248–50.

55. The Meriam report, in discussing Indian agriculture, stressed this point especially. See Lewis Meriam *et al.*, *The Problem of Indian Administration* (Baltimore, 1928), pp. 7, 460.

## VII. THE APPLICATION OF ALLOTMENT

1. *Lake Mohonk Conference Proceedings*, 1887, p. 67.

2. *Ibid.*, 1890, p. 81.

3. See above, pp. 13, 14–15.

4. *Report of the Commissioner of Indian Affairs*, 1891, p. 46.
5. *Ibid.*, 1890, p. xxxviii.
6. *Ibid.*, 1888, pp. 294, 302, 320, 322, 335–36, 340–44.
7. *Ibid.*, 1889, pp. 421, 432, 440, 447, 460, 463, 464.
8. *Lake Mohonk Conference Proceedings*, 1891, p. 14.
9. *Ibid.*, 1889, p. 9.
10. *Report of the Commissioner of Indian Affairs*, 1890, p. xxxix.
11. *Ibid.*, pp. xxxvii, xl.
12. *Ibid.*, 1888, p. xxxviii.
13. *Ibid.*, 1916, Table 6, p. 94.
14. *Ibid.; ibid.*, 1892, p. 184.
15. *Lake Mohonk Conference Proceedings*, 1892, p. 17.
16. *Report of the Commissioner of Indian Affairs*, 1893, p. 23; *ibid.*, 1894, p. 20; *ibid.*, 1895, p. 19; *ibid.*, 1896, p. 25; *ibid.*, 1897, p. 21; *ibid.*, 1898, p. 40; *ibid.*, 1899, p. 43; *ibid.*, 1900, pp. 53–54.
17. *Ibid.*, 1916, pp. 93–94.
18. *Ibid.*, 1891, p. 44; *ibid.*, 1892, p. 81.
19. Statistics compiled by the Land Division of the Indian Office.
20. *Report of the Board of Indian Commissioners*, 1890, p. 9.
21. *Report of the Commissioner of Indian Affairs*, 1890, pp. 512–14; *ibid.*, 1900, pp. 743–45.
22. *Report of the Indian Rights Association*, 1900, p. 57. This report lists the agencies as 56 in 1900, but the *Report of the Commissioner of Indian Affairs*, 1900, lists 61. See pp. 743–45.
23. See *Report of the Commissioner of Indian Affairs*, 1887, pp. 92, 93, 121–23, 135, 228; *ibid.*, 1888, pp. 25, 34, 50, 56, 70, 87, 109, 111, 151, 183, 204, 208, 211, 212, 238, 243; *ibid.*, 1889, pp. 172, 182, 197, 199, 217, 223, 251, 273, 297; *Report of the Board of Indian Commissioners*, 1889, p. 152; *ibid.*, 1891, pp. 13–14; *Report of the Commissioner of Indian Affairs*, 1892, pp. 296, 350, 403, 419, 517.
24. *Report of the Board of Indian Commissioners*, 1889, p. 9.
25. *Report of the Commissioner of Indian Affairs*, 1888, p. 208.
26. *Ibid.*, p. 70.
27. *Ibid.*, 1887, pp. 92–93.
28. *Report of the Board of Indian Commissioners*, 1891, pp. 13–14.
29. *Report of the Commissioner of Indian Affairs*, 1892, p. 391.
30. *Lake Mohonk Conference Proceedings*, 1890, p. 13.
31. *Ibid.*, pp. 81–82.
32. *Report of the Commissioner of Indian Affairs*, 1888, pp. 69, 70, 99, 111, 240; *ibid.*, 1889, pp. 143, 186, 192, 200, 214, 230, 250, 268, 297; *ibid.*, 1890, pp. 23, 28, 108, 129, 190, 194, 231, 225; *ibid.*, 1892, pp. 299, 330, 399, 403, 486; *ibid.*, 1900, pp. 233, 305, 381.
33. See above, pp. 37–38.
34. *Report of the Commissioner of Indian Affairs*, 1887, p. x.

35. *Ibid.*, p. 123; *ibid.*, 1889, pp. 20, 217; *ibid.*, 1890, p. xlvi.

36. *Lake Mohonk Conference Proceedings*, 1889, p. 42.

37. *Report of the Board of Indian Commissioners*, 1890, p. 27. The Osage population was about 1,500 in 1890, which would allow for an average of about 166 acres of arable land per capita.

38. *Report of the Commissioner of Indian Affairs*, 1887, p. 140. See also *ibid.*, 1889, p. 217.

39. *Ibid.*, p. 205.

40. *Ibid.*, p. 20. See also *Report of the Board of Indian Commissioners*, 1890, p. 27.

41. *Report of the Commissioner of Indian Affairs*, 1887, pp. 116–17.

42. *Ibid.*, pp. x–xiii.

43. See above, p. 44; *Report of the Commissioner of Indian Affairs*, 1892, pp. 250–52.

44. *Ibid.*, 1887, p. 117.

45. *Ibid.*, 1888, p. 135.

46. See Women's National Indian Association, *The Omaha Mission* (Philadelphia, 1888), p. 1; *Report of the Commissioner of Indian Affairs*, 1888, p. 92; *ibid.*, 1889, pp. 182, 230; *ibid.*, 1890, p. 31; *ibid.*, 1892, pp. 294, 457; *ibid.*, 1895, p. 255; *ibid.*, 1900, pp. 233, 381.

47. *Report of the Board of Indian Commissioners*, 1891, p. 16.

48. *Report of the Commissioner of Indian Affairs*, 1888, p. 99.

49. *Ibid.*, 1892, p. 393. See also *ibid.*, 1890, pp. 194, 225, 231.

50. *Ibid.*, 1888, p. 70.

51. "Affairs of the Mexican Kickapoo Indians: Hearings before the Subcommittee of the Committee on Indian Affairs, United States Senate," *Senate Document* No. 215, 60 Congress, 1 session, serial 5247, pp. 86, 249; serial 5248, pp. 1621, 1641, 1651, 1655; serial 5249, p. 1888.

52. *United States Statutes at Large*, XXVII, 557–59.

53. *Report of the Commissioner of Indian Affairs*, 1889, p. 195.

## VIII. ADMINISTRATION AND CHANGES IN POLICY: LEASING

1. *Report of the Commissioner of Indian Affairs*, 1889, p. 289.

2. *Ibid.*, 1888, p. 29. See also *ibid.*, p. 70; *ibid.*, 1889, p. 204; *ibid.*, 1890, p. 164.

3. *Ibid.*, 1889, p. 152.

4. *Lake Mohonk Conference Proceedings*, 1887, p. 99.

5. *Report of the Board of Indian Commissioners*, 1889, p. 153.

6. *Lake Mohonk Conference Proceedings*, 1889, p. 121.

7. *Report of the Commissioner of Indian Affairs*, 1891, p. 43.

8. *Lake Mohonk Conference Proceedings*, 1889, pp. 84–89.

9. *Ibid.*, p. 89.

10. *Report of the Board of Indian Commissioners*, 1890, p. 175.

11. *Lake Mohonk Conference Proceedings*, 1890, p. 138. See also *ibid.*, 1889, p. 96.

12. *Ibid.*, 1890, p. 138.

13. *Ibid.*, pp. 93–94. See also *Report of the Commissioner of Indian Affairs*, 1891, p. 149.

14. *Lake Mohonk Conference Proceedings*, 1889, p. 86. See also *ibid.*, 1890, p. 84.

15. *United States Statutes at Large*, XXV, 234.

16. *Report of the Commissioner of Indian Affairs*, 1888, p. 444.

17. *Report of the Board of Indian Commissioners*, 1888, p. 6.

18. *United States Statutes at Large*, XXV, 998; XXVI, 1007; XXVII, 137, 630.

19. *Report of the Commissioner of Indian Affairs*, 1890, p. 187. See also *ibid.*, p. 7.

20. *Ibid.*, 1892, p. 321.

21. *Ibid.*, 1888, p. 29; *ibid.*, 1892, p. 443; *ibid.*, 1893, pp. 338, 339; *ibid.*, 1899, p. 326.

22. *United States Statutes at Large*, X, 1044; XIV, 667.

23. Alice C. Fletcher and Francis LaFlesche, *The Omaha Tribe* (Twenty-seventh Annual Report of the Bureau of American Ethnology, Washington, 1911), pp. 623–24.

24. *Ibid.*, p. 637.

25. *Lake Mohonk Conference Proceedings*, 1889, pp. 103–104; *Report of the Board of Indian Commissioners*, 1889, pp. 148–49.

26. *Lake Mohonk Conference Proceedings*, 1890, p. 113.

27. *Ibid.*, 1889, p. 98.

28. *Ibid.*, p. 37.

29. *Ibid.*, p. 108; *ibid.*, 1890, p. 112.

30. *Ibid.*, 1891, pp. 74–76.

31. *Ibid.*, pp. 112–13.

32. Laurence F. Schmeckebier, *The Office of Indian Affairs: Its History, Activities, and Organization* (Baltimore, 1927), pp. 84, 84n.

33. *Lake Mohonk Conference Proceedings*, 1889, pp. 89–93.

34. *Ibid.*, pp. 108–109.

35. *Ibid.*, 1890, p. 85; *Report of the Board of Indian Commissioners*, 1894, p. 7.

36. *United States Statutes at Large*, XXVII, 63.

37. *Ibid.*, XLIV, part 2, 174; XLV, part 1, 899.

38. Mr. Dodd and Mr. Govern of the Indian Office Finance and Fiscal Divisions, respectively, knew of no similar legislation.

39. *Report of the Commissioner of Indian Affairs,* 1889, p. 17.
40. *Report of the Board of Indian Commissioners,* 1889, p. 8.
41. *Ibid.,* p. 9.
42. *Lake Mohonk Conference Proceedings,* 1889, pp. 84–89.
43. *Ibid.,* p. 94.
44. *Ibid.,* pp. 94–97.
45. *Report of the Commissioner of Indian Affairs,* 1890, p. 137.
46. *Lake Mohonk Conference Proceedings,* 1889, p. 87.
47. *Ibid.,* 1890, pp. 82–83.
48. *Ibid.,* p. 105.
49. *Ibid.,* p. 110.
50. *Report of the Indian Rights Association,* 1890, pp. 9–10.
51. *Report of the Commissioner of Indian Affairs,* 1888, pp. xxxix–xl.

52. The criticism directed at the Commissioner especially by the Indian Rights Association was claimed by the organization to be the cause of the Commissioner's dismissal and of the appointment of J. H. Oberly in his place. *Report of the Indian Rights Association,* 1889, pp. 9–10.
53. See above, p. 107.
54. See above, p. 106.
55. *Senate Executive Document* No. 64, 51 Congress, 1 session, serial 2686, pp. 1–4.
56. *Congressional Record,* XXI, 2068 (March 10, 1890).
57. See above, pp. 108–109.
58. Copy of bill in Senate Document Room files.
59. *Ibid.*
60. *House Report* No. 1809, 51 Congress, 1 session, serial 2812.
61. *Ibid.* See *Lake Mohonk Conference Proceedings,* 1890, p. 105.
62. *Congressional Record,* XXI, 10705–706 (September 29, 1890); *ibid.,* 10710 (September 30, 1890); *ibid.,* XXII, 3118, 3152 (February 23, 1891).
63. *United States Statutes at Large,* XXVI, 794–96.
64. *Congressional Record,* XXI, 10705 (September 29, 1890).
65. *House Report* No. 1700, 51 Congress, 1 session, serial 2812.
66. *Report of the Indian Rights Association,* 1890, pp. 9–10.
67. *Report of the Commissioner of Indian Affairs,* 1890, pp. xlviii–xlix.
68. *Lake Mohonk Conference Proceedings,* 1891, pp. 12–14, 112–14.
69. See comments on legislation in *Report of the Indian Rights Association,* 1891.
70. See above, p. 108–109.
71. *Lake Mohonk Conference Proceedings,* 1891, pp. 87–88.

72. *Report of the Commissioner of Indian Affairs*, 1892, p. 404.
73. *Ibid.*, p. 504; *ibid.*, 1893, pp. 248, 339; *ibid.*, 1894, p. 136.
74. *Ibid.*, 1892, p. 188.
75. *Ibid.*, p. 71.
76. *Ibid.*, p. 72.
77. *Ibid.*, 1893, p. 476.
78. *Ibid.*, p. 27.
79. *Congressional Record*, XXII, 3118 (February 23, 1891).
80. *Report of the Commissioner of Indian Affairs*, 1893, p. 27.
81. *Ibid.*, 1894, p. 234.
82. *United States Statutes at Large*, XXVIII, 305.
83. *Report of the Commissioner of Indian Affairs*, 1894, p. 33.
84. *Ibid.*, p. 421.
85. *Report of the Board of Indian Commissioners*, 1894, p. 7. See also *Lake Mohonk Conference Proceedings*, 1894, pp. 17–18; *Report of the Commissioner of Indian Affairs*, 1894, p. 33.
86. *Lake Mohonk Conference Proceedings*, 1894, pp. 86–87. See also *Report of the Indian Rights Association*, 1894, pp. 36–38.
87. *Lake Mohonk Conference Proceedings*, 1894, pp. 87–88.
88. *Ibid.*, p. 149.
89. *Report of the Indian Rights Association*, 1894, p. 38.
90. *Report of the Commissioner of Indian Affairs*, 1896, p. 42.
91. *Report of the Board of Indian Commissioners*, 1895, pp. 7–8.
92. *Report of the Commissioner of Indian Affairs*, 1894, p. 33; *ibid.*, 1895, pp. 34–35; *ibid.*, 1896, pp. 39–42; *ibid.*, 1897, pp. 41–43.
93. *United States Statutes at Large*, XXX, 85.
94. *Report of the Commissioner of Indian Affairs*, 1897, pp. 40–43.
95. *Report of the Indian Rights Association*, 1897, pp. 22–27.
96. *Report of the Commissioner of Indian Affairs*, 1897, pp. 41–43; *ibid.*, 1898, p. 61.
97. *Ibid.*, 1899, p. 60; *ibid.*, 1900, pp. 76–78.
98. *United States Statutes at Large*, XXXI, 229.
99. *Report of the Board of Indian Commissioners*, 1900, pp. 16, 17; *Lake Mohonk Conference Proceedings*, 1900, pp. 7–8; *Report of the Indian Rights Association*, 1900, pp. 58–59.
100. *Report of the Commissioner of Indian Affairs*, 1900, p. 13.
101. *Report of the Indian Rights Association*, 1900, p. 58.

## IX. RESULTS OF ALLOTMENT TO 1900

1. *Report of the Board of Indian Commissioners*, 1890, pp. 31–32.
2. *Report of the Commissioner of Indian Affairs*, 1895, pp. 260, 262, 335.

3. *Report of the Board of Indian Commissioners,* 1898, p. 3. See also the agent's comments in *Report of the Commissioner of Indian Affairs,* 1892, p. 190.
4. *Ibid.,* 1895, p. 302. See also *ibid.,* p. 260.
5. *Report of the Board of Indian Commissioners,* 1898, p. 14.
6. *Ibid.,* p. 18. See also *ibid.,* p. 15; *Report of the Commissioner of Indian Affairs,* 1900, p. 361.
7. *Ibid.,* 1896, p. 272.
8. *Ibid.,* 1894, p. 253.
9. *Lake Mohonk Conference Proceedings,* 1890, p. 82.
10. *Report of the Board of Indian Commissioners,* 1898, p. 24.
11. *Ibid.,* 1899, p. 19.
12. *Report of the Commissioner of Indian Affairs,* 1900, p. 13. See above, pp. 121–22.
13. *Report of the Commissioner of Indian Affairs,* 1892, p. 190; *ibid.,* 1896, p. 272.
14. *Ibid.,* 1894, p. 136.
15. *Ibid.,* 1895, p. 150.
16. *Ibid.,* 1896, p. 149.
17. *Ibid.,* 1893, pp. 193, 195. See also *ibid.,* 1892, p. 186.
18. *Report of the Indian Rights Association,* 1894, pp. 37, 38.
19. *Lake Mohonk Conference Proceedings,* 1894, pp. 86–87.
20. *Report of the Commissioner of Indian Affairs,* 1895, pp. 37–38.
21. *Ibid.,* 1894, pp. 187–88.
22. *Ibid.,* 1895, pp. 37–41.
23. *Ibid.,* 1894, p. 188.
24. *Ibid.,* 1895, p. 41.
25. Margaret Mead, *The Changing Culture of an Indian Tribe* (New York, 1932), p. 27.
26. *Report of the Board of Indian Commissioners,* 1898, p. 25.
27. *Ibid.,* 1891, p. 144.
28. Alice C. Fletcher and Francis LaFlesche, *The Omaha Tribe* (Twenty-seventh Annual Report of the Bureau of American Ethnology, Washington, 1911), p. 640.
29. *Report of the Commissioner of Indian Affairs,* 1891, p. 38.
30. *Ibid.,* 1892, pp. 185–95.
31. *Report of the Board of Indian Commissioners,* 1898, pp. 12–25; *ibid.,* 1899, pp. 8–13, 30–75.
32. *Ibid.,* 1898, p. 13.
33. *Ibid.,* pp. 22–23.
34. *Ibid.,* p. 18.
35. *Ibid.,* p. 17.
36. *Ibid.,* pp. 15–21; *ibid.,* 1899, pp. 30–75. See also *Report of the Commissioner of Indian Affairs,* 1892, pp. 185, 504; *ibid.,* 1895, p. 149.

37. *Report of the Board of Indian Commissioners*, 1898, p. 13. See also *ibid.*, p. 22.
38. *Ibid.*, 1899, pp. 10–12.
39. *Ibid.*, 1898, p. 12.
40. *Ibid.*, p. 25.
41. *Report of the Commissioner of Indian Affairs*, 1892, p. 306; *ibid.*, 1896, p. 197.
42. *Ibid.*, 1895, p. 318.
43. *Ibid.*, p. 243.
44. *Ibid.*, 1894, p. 337.
45. *Ibid.*, 1895, p. 261.
46. *Ibid.*, 1895, p. 403.
47. *Ibid.*, 1890, p. 480; *ibid.*, 1900, p. 677.
48. See above, pp. 134–35.
49. *Report of the Commissioner of Indian Affairs*, 1890, p. xxxix.
50. *Report of the Board of Indian Commissioners*, 1890, p. 9.
51. *Lake Mohonk Conference Proceedings*, 1889, p. 84.
52. *Ibid.*, p. 68.
53. *Report of the Board of Indian Commissioners*, 1890, p. 12.
54. *Lake Mohonk Conference Proceedings*, 1889, pp. 85, 86.
55. *Ibid.*, 1891, p. 83.
56. *Report of the Board of Indian Commissioners*, 1889, p. 150.
57. *Ibid.*, 1898, p. 14.
58. *Lake Mohonk Conference Proceedings*, 1890, p. 116.
59. *Report of the Commissioner of Indian Affairs*, 1894, p. 269.
60. See Warren K. Moorehead, *The American Indian in the United States* (Andover, Massachusetts, 1914), pp. 59, 62, 71 ff.
61. *Report of the Commissioner of Indian Affairs*, 1888, p. xxxviii.
62. *Lake Mohonk Conference Proceedings*, 1894, p. 86.
63. *Report of the Indian Rights Association*, 1894, pp. 36–37.
64. *Report of the Commissioner of Indian Affairs*, 1895, p. 22.
65. Flora Warren Seymour, *The Story of the Red Man* (New York, 1929), p. 376; letter from Mrs. Seymour to the writer.
66. Information from Mr. Roblin.
67. See above, p. 139.
68. *Report of the Board of Indian Commissioners*, 1898, pp. 12–25; *ibid.*, 1899, pp. 30–75.
69. *Report of the Commissioner of Indian Affairs*, 1916, p. 112.
70. See above, p. 109.
71. *Lake Mohonk Conference Proceedings*, 1890, p. 82.
72. *Ibid.*, p. 146.
73. *Report of the Board of Indian Commissioners*, 1898, p. 15.
74. *United States Statutes at Large*, XXXIV, 182.
75. *Ibid.*, XXVII, 633; XXVIII, 295.

76. *Report of the Indian Rights Association*, 1894, p. 38; *Report of the Board of Indian Commissioners*, 1894, p. 8; *Lake Mohonk Conference Proceedings*, 1894, pp. 17–18.

77. George Bird Grinnell, *The Indians of To-day* (New York, 1900), p. 167. See also *ibid.*, pp. 168–70; *Report of the Commissioner of Indian Affairs*, 1900, p. 448.

78. *Lake Mohonk Conference Proceedings*, 1896, pp. 11–12.

79. See above, p. 58.

80. *Report of the Board of Indian Commissioners*, 1899, p. 19.

81. *Lake Mohonk Conference Proceedings*, 1889, p. 45.

# APPENDIX A

## DAWES ACT, 1887

An act to provide for the allotment of lands in severalty to Indians on the various reservations, and to extend the protection of the laws of the United States and the Territories over the Indians, and for other purposes.

*Be it enacted by the Senate and House of Representatives of the United States of America in Congress assembled,* That in all cases where any tribe or band of Indians has been, or shall hereafter be, located upon any reservation created for their use, either by treaty stipulation or by virtue of an act of Congress or executive order setting apart the same for their use, the President of the United States be, and he hereby is, authorized, whenever in his opinion any reservation or any part thereof of such Indians is advantageous for agricultural and grazing purposes, to cause said reservation, or any part thereof, to be surveyed, or resurveyed if necessary, and to allot the lands in said reservation in severalty to any Indian located thereon in quantities as follows:

To each head of a family, one-quarter of a section;

To each single person over eighteen years of age, one-eighth of a section;

To each orphan child under eighteen years of age, one-eighth of a section; and

To each other single person under eighteen years now living, or who may be born prior to the date of the order of the President directing an allotment of the lands embraced in any reservation, one-sixteenth of a section: *Provided,* That in case there is not sufficient land in any of said reservations to allot lands to each individual of the classes above named in quantities as above provided, the lands embraced in such reservation or reservations shall be allotted to each individual of each of said classes pro rata in accordance with the provisions of this act: *And provided further,* That where the treaty or act of Congress setting apart such reservation provides for the allotment of lands in severalty in quantities in excess of those herein provided, the President, in making allotments upon such reservation, shall allot the lands to each individual Indian belonging thereon in quantity as specified in such treaty or act: *And provided further,* That when the lands allotted are only valuable for grazing purposes, an additional allotment of such grazing lands, in quantities as above provided, shall be made to each individual.

Sec. 2. That all allotments set apart under the provisions of this act shall be selected by the Indians, heads of families selecting for their minor children, and the agents shall select for each orphan child, and in such manner as to embrace the improvements of the Indians making the selection. Where the improvements of two or more Indians have been made on the same legal subdivision of land, unless they shall otherwise agree, a provisional line may be run dividing said lands between them, and the amount to which each is entitled shall be equalized in the assignment of the remainder of the land to which they are entitled under this act: *Provided,* That if any one entitled to an allotment shall fail to make a selection within four years after the President shall direct that allotments may be made on a particular reservation, the Secretary of the Interior may direct the agent of such tribe or band, if such there be, and if there be no agent, then a special agent appointed for that purpose, to make a selection for such Indian, which selection shall be allotted as in cases where selections are made by the Indians, and patents shall issue in like manner.

Sec. 3. That the allotments provided for in this act shall be made by special agents appointed by the President for such purpose, and the agents in charge of the respective reservations on which the allotments are directed to be made, under such rules and regulations as the Secretary of the Interior may from time to time prescribe, and shall be certified by such agents to the Commissioner of Indian Affairs, in duplicate, one copy to be retained in the Indian Office and the other to be transmitted to the Secretary of the Interior for his action, and to be deposited in the General Land Office.

Sec. 4. That where any Indian not residing upon a reservation, or for whose tribe no reservation has been provided by treaty, act of Congress, or executive order, shall make settlement upon any surveyed or unsurveyed lands of the United States not otherwise appropriated, he or she shall be entitled, upon application to the local land office for the district in which the lands are located, to have the same allotted to him or her, and to his or her children, in quantities and manner as provided in this act for Indians residing upon reservations; and when such settlement is made upon unsurveyed lands, the grant to such Indians shall be adjusted upon the survey of the lands so as to conform thereto; and patents shall be issued to them for such lands in the manner and with the restrictions as herein provided. And the fees to which the officers of such local land office would have been entitled had such lands been entered under the general laws for the disposition of the public lands shall be paid to them, from any moneys in the Treasury of the United States not otherwise appropriated, upon a statement of an account in their behalf for such fees by the Commissioner of the General Land Office, and a certification of such account to the Secretary of the Treasury by the Secretary of the Interior.

Sec. 5. That upon the approval of the allotments provided for in this act by the Secretary of the Interior, he shall cause patents to issue therefor in the name of the allottees, which patents shall be of the legal effect, and declare that the United States does and will hold the land thus allotted, for the period of twenty-five years, in trust for the sole use and benefit of the Indian to whom such allotment shall have been made, or, in case of his decease, of his heirs according to the laws of the State or Territory where such land is located, and that at the expiration of said period the United States will convey the same by patent to said Indian, or his heirs as aforesaid, in fee, discharged of said trust and free of all charge or incumbrance whatsoever: *Provided*, That the President of the United States may in any case in his discretion extend the period. And if any conveyance shall be made of the lands set apart and allotted as herein provided, or any contract made touching the same, before the expiration of the time above mentioned, such conveyance or contract shall be absolutely null and void: *Provided*, That the law of descent and partition in force in the State or Territory where such lands are situate shall apply thereto after patents therefor have been executed and delivered, except as herein otherwise provided; and the laws of the State of Kansas regulating the descent and partition of real estate shall, so far as practicable, apply to all lands in the Indian Territory which may be allotted in severalty under the provisions of this act: *And provided further*, That at any time after lands have been allotted to all the Indians of any tribe as herein provided, or sooner if in the opinion of the

President it shall be for the best interests of said tribe, it shall be lawful for the Secretary of the Interior to negotiate with such Indian tribe for the purchase and release by said tribe, in conformity with the treaty or statute under which such reservation is held, of such portions of its reservation not allotted as such tribe shall, from time to time, consent to sell, on such terms and conditions as shall be considered just and equitable between the United States and said tribe of Indians, which purchase shall not be complete until ratified by Congress, and the form and manner of executing such release shall also be prescribed by Congress: *Provided however*, That all lands adapted to agriculture, with or without irrigation so sold or released to the United States by any Indian tribe shall be held by the United States for the sole purpose of securing homes to actual settlers and shall be disposed of by the United States to actual and bona fide settlers only in tracts not exceeding one hundred and sixty acres to any one person, on such terms as Congress shall prescribe, subject to grants which Congress may make in aid of education: *And provided further*, That no patents shall issue therefor except to the person so taking the same as and for a homestead, or his heirs, and after the expiration of five years occupancy thereof as such homestead; and any conveyance of said lands so taken as a homestead, or any contract touching the same, or lien thereon, created prior to the date of such patent, shall be null and void. And the sums agreed to be paid by the United States as purchase money for any portion of any such reservation shall be held in the Treasury of the United States for the sole use of the tribe or tribes of Indians to whom such reservations belonged; and the same, with interest thereon at three per cent per annum, shall be at all times subject to appropriation by Congress for the education and civilization of such tribe or tribes of Indians or the members thereof. The patents aforesaid shall be recorded in the General Land

Office, and afterward delivered, free of charge, to the allottee entitled thereto. And if any religious society or other organization is now occupying any of the public lands to which this act is applicable, for religious or educational work among the Indians, the Secretary of the Interior is hereby authorized to confirm such occupation to such society or organization, in quantity not exceeding one hundred and sixty acres in any one tract, so long as the same shall be so occupied, on such terms as he shall deem just; but nothing herein contained shall change or alter any claim of such society for religious or educational purposes heretofore granted by law. And hereafter in the employment of Indian police, or any other employes in the public service among any of the Indian tribes or bands affected by this act, and where Indians can perform the duties required, those Indians who have availed themselves of the provisions of this act and become citizens of the United States shall be preferred.

Sec. 6. That upon the completion of said allotments and the patenting of the lands to said allottees, each and every member of the respective bands or tribes of Indians to whom allotments have been made shall have the benefit of and be subject to the laws, both civil and criminal, of the State or Territory in which they may reside; and no Territory shall pass or enforce any law denying any such Indian within its jurisdiction the equal protection of the law. And every Indian born within the territorial limits of the United States to whom allotments shall have been made under the provisions of this act, or under any law or treaty, and every Indian born within the territorial limits of the United States who has voluntarily taken up, within said limits, his residence separate and apart from any tribe of Indians therein, and has adopted the habits of civilized life, is hereby declared to be a citizen of the United States, and is entitled to all the rights, privileges, and immunities of such citizens, whether said Indian has been or not, by birth or otherwise, a member of any tribe of Indians within the territorial limits of the United States without in any manner impairing or otherwise affecting the right of any such Indian to tribal or other property.

Sec. 7. That in cases where the use of water for irrigation is necessary to render the lands within any Indian reservation available for agricultural purposes, the Secretary of the Interior be, and he is hereby, authorized to prescribe such rules and regulations as he may deem necessary to secure a just and equal distribution thereof among the Indians residing upon any such reservations; and no other appropriation or grant of water by any riparian proprietor shall be authorized or permitted to the damage of any other riparian proprietor.

Sec. 8. That the provision of this act shall not extend to the territory occupied by the Cherokees, Creeks, Choctaws, Chickasaws, Seminoles, and Osage, Miamies and Peorias, and Sacs and Foxes, in the Indian Territory, nor to any of the reservations of the Seneca Nation of New York Indians in the State of New York, nor to that strip of territory in the State of Nebraska adjoining the Sioux Nation on the south added by executive order.

Sec. 9. That for the purpose of making the surveys and resurveys mentioned in section two of this act, there be, and hereby is, appropriated, out of any moneys in the Treasury not otherwise appropriated, the sum of one hundred thousand dollars, to be repaid proportionately out of the proceeds of the sales of such land as may be acquired from the Indians under the provisions of this act.

Sec. 10. That nothing in this act contained shall be so construed as to affect the right and power of Congress to grant the right of way through any lands granted to an Indian, or a tribe of Indians, for railroads or other highways, or telegraph lines, for the public use, or to condemn such lands to public uses, upon making just compensation.

Sec. 11. That nothing in this act shall be so construed as to prevent the removal of the Southern Ute Indians from their present reservation in Southwestern Colorado to a new reservation by and with the consent of a majority of the adult male members of said tribe.

Approved, February 8, 1887.

*United States Statutes at Large,* XXIV, 388-91

# APPENDIX B

## ACT OF 1891

An act to amend and further extend the benefits of the act approved February eighth, eighteen hundred and eighty-seven, entitled "An act to provide for the allotment of land in severalty to Indians on the various reservations, and to extend the protection of the laws of the United States over the Indians, and for other purposes."

*Be it enacted by the Senate and House of Representatives of the United States of America in Congress assembled,* That section one of the act entitled "An act to provide for the allotment of lands in severalty to Indians on the various reservations, and to extend the protection of the laws of the United States and the Territories over the Indians, and for other purposes," approved February eighth, eighteen hundred and eighty-seven, be, and the same is hereby, amended so as to read as follows:

"Sec. 1. That in all cases where any tribe or band of Indians has been, or shall hereafter be, located upon any reservation created for their use, either by treaty stipulation or by virtue of an Act of Congress or Executive order setting apart the same for their use, the President of the United

States be, and he hereby is, authorized, whenever in his opinion any reservation, or any part thereof, of such Indians is advantageous for agricultural or grazing purposes, to cause said reservation, or any part thereof, to be surveyed, or resurveyed, if necessary, and to allot to each Indian located thereon one-eighth of a section of land: *Provided,* That in case there is not sufficient land in any of said reservations to allot lands to each individual in quantity as above provided the land in such reservation or reservations shall be allotted to each individual pro rata, as near as may be, according to legal subdivisions: *Provided further,* That where the treaty or act of Congress setting apart such reservation provides for the allotment of lands in severalty to certain classes in quantity in excess of that herein provided the President, in making allotments upon such reservation, shall allot the land to each individual Indian of said classes belonging thereon in quantity as specified in such treaty or act, and to other Indians belonging thereon in quantity as herein provided: *Provided further,* That where existing agreements or laws provide for allotments in accordance with the provisions of said act of February eighth, eighteen hundred and eighty-seven, or in quantities substantially as therein provided, allotments may be made in quantity as specified in this act, with the consent of the Indians, expressed in such manner as the President, in his discretion, may require: *And provided further,* That when the lands allotted, or any legal subdivision thereof, are only valuable for grazing purposes, such lands shall be allotted in double quantities."

Sec. 2. That where allotments have been made in whole or in part upon any reservation under the provisions of said act of February eighth, eighteen hundred and eighty-seven, and the quantity of land in such reservation is sufficient to give each member of the tribe eighty acres, such allotments shall be revised and equalized under the provisions of this act: *Provided*, That no allotment heretofore approved by the Secretary of the Interior shall be reduced in quantity.

Sec. 3. That whenever it shall be made to appear to the Secretary of the Interior that, by reason of age or other disability, any allottee under the provisions of said act, or any other act or treaty can not personally and with benefit to himself occupy or improve his allotment or any part thereof the same may be leased upon such terms, regulations and conditions as shall be prescribed by such Secretary, for a term not exceeding three years for farming or grazing, or ten years for mining purposes: *Provided*, That where lands are occupied by Indians who have bought and paid for the same, and which lands are not needed for farming or agricultural purposes, and are not desired for individual allotments, the same may be leased by authority of the Council speaking for such Indians, for a period not to exceed five years for grazing, or ten years for mining purposes in such quantities and upon such terms and conditions as the agent in charge of such reservation may recommend, subject to the approval of the Secretary of the Interior.

Sec. 4. That where any Indian entitled to allotment under existing laws shall make settlement upon any surveyed or unsurveyed lands of the United States not otherwise appropriated, he or she shall be entitled, upon application to the local land office for the district in which the lands are located, to have the same allotted to him or her and to his or her children, in quantities and manner as provided in the foregoing section of this amending act for Indians residing upon reservations; and when such settlement is made upon unsurveyed lands the grant to such Indians shall be adjusted upon the survey of the lands so as to conform thereto; and patents shall be issued to them for such lands in the manner and with the restrictions provided in the act to which this is an amendment. And the fees to which the officers of such local land office would have been entitled had such lands been entered under the general laws for the disposition of the public lands shall be paid to them from any moneys in the Treasury of the United States not otherwise appropriated, upon a statement of an account in their behalf for such fees by the Commissioner of the General Land Office, and a certification of such account to the Secretary of the Treasury by the Secretary of the Interior.

Sec. 5. That for the purpose of determining the descent of land to the heirs of any deceased Indian under the provisions of the fifth section of said act, whenever any male and female Indian shall have co-habited together as husband and wife according to the custom and manner of Indian life the issue of such co-habitation shall be, for the purpose aforesaid, taken and deemed to be the legitimate issue of the Indians so living together, and every Indian child, otherwise illegitimate, shall for such purpose be taken and deemed to be the legitimate issue of the father of such child: *Provided*, That the provisions of this act shall not be held or construed as to apply to the lands commonly called and known as the "Cherokee Outlet": *And provided further*, That no allotment of lands shall be made or annuities of money paid to any of the Sac and Fox of the Missouri Indians who were not enrolled as members of said tribe on January first, eighteen hundred and ninety; but this shall not be held to impair or otherwise affect the rights or equities of any person whose claim to membership in said tribe is now pending and being investigated.

Approved, February 28, 1891.

*United States Statutes at Large*, XXVI, 794–96.

# INDEX

Abbott, Rev. Lyman: 29, 58, 154
Absentee Shawnee Indians: 92,
    151
Act of 1887: *see* Dawes Act
Act of 1891, text of: 185–88; *see
    also* leasing of allotments
Act of 1906: *see* Burke Act
Adult education: *see* agricultural
    training
Agencies: *see* Indian agencies
Agents: *see* Indian agents
Agricultural training: 61, 69–71,
    77–81, 101–102
Agriculture: *see* Indian agricul-
    ture
Aims of allotment policy: 8–32
Alienation of Indian lands: 6, 7,
    13, 50–51, 150–51
Allotment of land in severalty:
    historical works on, xv;
    history of, 3–7; aims of pro-
    moters, 8–32; reformers' sup-
    port of, 34–39; opposition to,
    18–19, 37–38; Indian atti-
    tudes on, 40–56, 88–97;
    evaluation of, 46–56, 98–99,
    124–55; as civilizing agent, 56,
    66–67, 69, 98; application of,
    82–88; equalization of, 106–
    107, 110–13; white interest in,

141–48; *see also* leasing of
    allotments
Allotments: statistics on, 86–87,
    138–40; freedom from taxes,
    105–106
American Bureau of Ethnology:
    38
American Indian Defense Associ-
    ation: xii
*American Indians*: xvi
American Institute of Instruc-
    tion: 168
Americanization of Indians: 75,
    81
Annuities: 76
Anti-Saloon League: 35
Apache Indians: 48
Arapaho Indians: *see* Cheyenne
    and Arapaho Indians
Armstrong, Samuel C.: 66–67,
    99, 105
Assimilation of Indians: ix, 67
Atkins, J. D. C., Commissioner
    of Indian Affairs: 5, 24, 43–44,
    45, 49, 52–53, 59–60, 62,
    91–92, 94
Attorney General: 110
Ayres, Congressman William A.:
    xii, xiv

Winnebago agent: *see* Omaha
 and Winnebago agent
Winnebago Indians: 128–31,
 144–45
Wisconsin Indian Association:
 92–93, 150
Wisconsin State Republican
 Committee: 27

Woman's Christian Temperance
 Union: 34, 35
Women's National Indian
 Association: 33–34, 103, 162
Wright, Agent James G.: 45

Yakima agent: 41
Yankton agent: 9, 55, 89, 96

THE CIVILIZATION OF THE AMERICAN INDIAN SERIES
of which *The Dawes Act and the Allotment of Indian Land*
is the one hundred and twenty-third volume, was inaug-
urated in 1932 by the University of Oklahoma Press, and
has as its purpose the reconstruction of American Indian
civilization by presenting aboriginal, historical, and contemporary Indian life. The following list is complete as of
the date of printing of this volume:

1. Alfred Barnaby Thomas. *Forgotten Frontiers*: A Study
   of the Spanish Indian Policy of Don Juan Bautista de
   Anza, Governor of New Mexico, 1777–1787.
2. Grant Foreman. *Indian Removal*: The Emigration of
   the Five Civilized Tribes of Indians.
3. John Joseph Mathews. *Wah'Kon-Tah*: The Osage
   and the White Man's Road.
4. Grant Foreman. *Advancing the Frontier, 1830–1860*.
5. John Homer Seger. *Early Days among the Cheyenne
   and Arapahoe Indians*. Edited by Stanley Vestal.
6. Angie Debo. *The Rise and Fall of the Choctaw Republic*.
7. Stanley Vestal (ed.). *New Sources of Indian History,
   1850–1891*. Out of print.
8. Grant Foreman. *The Five Civilized Tribes*.
9. Alfred Barnaby Thomas. *After Coronado*: Spanish Ex-
   ploration Northeast of New Mexico, 1696–1727.
10. Frank G. Speck. *Naskapi*: The Savage Hunters of the
    Labrador Peninsula. Out of print.
11. Elaine Goodale Eastman. *Pratt*: The Red Man's
    Moses.
12. Althea Bass. *Cherokee Messenger*: A Life of Samuel
    Austin Worcester.
13. Thomas Wildcat Alford. *Civilization*. As told to Flor-
    ence Drake. Out of print.

14. Grant Foreman. *Indians and Pioneers:* The Story of the American Southwest before 1830.
15. George E. Hyde. *Red Cloud's Folk:* A History of the Oglala Sioux Indians.
16. Grant Foreman. *Sequoyah.*
17. Morris L. Wardell. *A Political History of the Cherokee Nation, 1838–1907.* Out of print.
18. John Walton Caughey. *McGillivray of the Creeks.* Out of print.
19. Edward Everett Dale and Gaston Litton. *Cherokee Cavaliers:* Forty Years of Cherokee History as Told in the Correspondence of the Ridge-Watie-Boudinot Family.
20. Ralph Henry Gabriel. *Elias Boudinot, Cherokee, and His America.* Out of print.
21. Karl N. Llewellyn and E. Adamson Hoebel. *The Cheyenne Way:* Conflicts and Case Law in Primitive Jurisprudence.
22. Angie Debo. *The Road to Disappearance.*
23. Oliver La Farge and others. *The Changing Indian.* Out of print.
24. Carolyn Thomas Foreman. *Indians Abroad.* Out of print.
25. John Adair. *The Navajo and Pueblo Silversmiths.*
26. Alice Marriott. *The Ten Grandmothers.*
27. Alice Marriott. *María:* The Potter of San Ildefonso.
28. Edward Everett Dale. *The Indians of the Southwest:* A Century of Development under the United States.
29. Adrián Recinos. *Popol Vuh:* The Sacred Book of the Ancient Quiché Maya. English version by Delia Goetz and Sylvanus G. Morley from the translation of Adrián Recinos.
30. Walter Collins O'Kane. *Sun in the Sky.*

31. Stanley A. Stubbs. *Bird's-Eye View of the Pueblos.* Out of print.
32. Katharine C. Turner. *Red Men Calling on the Great White Father.*
33. Muriel H. Wright. *A Guide to the Indian Tribes of Oklahoma.*
34. Ernest Wallace and E. Adamson Hoebel. *The Comanches:* Lords of the South Plains.
35. Walter Collins O'Kane. *The Hopis:* Portrait of a Desert People.
36. Joseph Epes Brown. *The Sacred Pipe:* Black Elk's Account of the Seven Rites of the Oglala Sioux.
37. Adrián Recinos and Delia Goetz (translators). *The Annals of the Cakchiquels.* Translated from the Cakchiquel Maya, with *Title of the Lords of Totonicapán,* translated from the Quiché text into Spanish by Dionisio José Chonay, English version by Delia Goetz.
38. R. S. Cotterill. *The Southern Indians:* The Story of the Civilized Tribes before Removal.
39. J. Eric S. Thompson. *The Rise and Fall of Maya Civilization.*
40. Robert Emmitt. *The Last War Trail:* The Utes and the Settlement of Colorado. Out of print.
41. Frank Gilbert Roe. *The Indian and the Horse.*
42. Francis Haines. *The Nez Percés:* Tribesmen of the Columbia Plateau.
43. Ruth M. Underhill. *The Navajos.*
44. George Bird Grinnell. *The Fighting Cheyennes.*
45. George E. Hyde. *A Sioux Chronicle.* Out of print.
46. Stanley Vestal. *Sitting Bull, Champion of the Sioux:* A Biography.
47. Edwin C. McReynolds. *The Seminoles.*
48. William T. Hagan. *The Sac and Fox Indians.*

49. John C. Ewers. *The Blackfeet:* Raiders on the Northwestern Plains. Out of print.
50. Alfonso Caso. *The Aztecs:* People of the Sun. Translated by Lowell Dunham.
51. C. L. Sonnichsen. *The Mescalero Apaches.*
52. Keith A. Murray. *The Modocs and Their War.*
53. Victor W. von Hagen (editor). *The Incas of Pedro de Cieza de León.* Translated by Harriet de Onis.
54. George E. Hyde. *Indians of the High Plains:* From the Prehistoric Period to the Coming of the Europeans.
55. George Catlin. *Episodes from "Life among the Indians" and "Last Rambles."* Edited by Marvin C. Ross. Out of print.
56. J. Eric S. Thompson. *Maya Hieroglyphic Writing:* An Introduction.
57. George E. Hyde. *Spotted Tail's Folk:* A History of the Brulé Sioux.
58. James Larpenteur Long. *The Assiniboines:* From the Accounts of the Old Ones Told to First Boy (James Larpenteur Long). Edited and with an introduction by Michael Stephen Kennedy. Out of print.
59. Edwin Thompson Denig. *Five Indian Tribes of the Upper Missouri.* Edited and with an introduction by John C. Ewers.
60. John Joseph Mathews. *The Osages:* Children of the Middle Waters.
61. Mary Elizabeth Young. *Redskins, Ruffleshirts, and Rednecks:* Indian Allotments in Alabama and Mississippi, 1830–1860.
62. J. Eric S. Thompson. *A Catalog of Maya Hieroglyphs.*
63. Mildred P. Mayhall. *The Kiowas.*
64. George E. Hyde. *Indians of the Woodlands:* From Prehistoric Times to 1725.

65. Grace Steele Woodward. *The Cherokees*.
66. Donald J. Berthrong. *The Southern Cheyennes*.
67. Miguel León-Portilla. *Aztec Thought and Culture: A Study of the Ancient Nahuatl Mind*.
68. T. D. Allen. *Navahos Have Five Fingers*.
69. Burr Cartwright Brundage. *Empire of the Inca*.
70. A. M. Gibson. *The Kickapoos*: Lords of the Middle Border.
71. Hamilton A. Tyler. *Pueblo Gods and Myths*.
72. Royal B. Hassrick. *The Sioux*: Life and Customs of a Warrior Society. Written in collaboration with Dorothy Maxwell and Cile M. Bach.
73. Franc Johnson Newcomb. *Hosteen Klah*: Navaho Medicine Man and Sand Painter.
74. Virginia Cole Trenholm and Maurine Carley. *The Shoshonis*: Sentinels of the Rockies.
75. Cohoe. *A Cheyenne Sketchbook*. Commentary by E. Adamson Hoebel and Karen Daniels Petersen. Out of print.
76. Jack D. Forbes. *Warriors of the Colorado*: The Quechans and Their Neighbors.
77. Ralph L. Roys (editor and translator). *Ritual of the Bacabs*.
78. Lillian Estelle Fisher. *The Last Inca Revolt*.
79. Lilly de Jongh Osborne. *Indian Crafts of Guatemala and El Salvador*.
80. Robert H. Ruby and John A. Brown. *Half-Sun on the Columbia*: A Biography of Chief Moses.
81. Jack Frederick and Anna Gritts Kilpatrick (editor and translators). *The Shadow of Sequoyah*: Social Documents of the Cherokees.
82. Ella E. Clark. *Indian Legends from the Northern Rockies*.

83. William A. Brophy and Sophie D. Aberle, M.D. (editors). *The Indian: America's Unfinished Business.*
84. M. Inez Hilger with Margaret A. Mondloch. *Huenun Ñamku: An Araucanian Indian of the Andes Remembers the Past.* Preface by Margaret Mead.
85. Ronald Spores. *The Mixtec Kings and Their People.*
86. David H. Corkran. *The Creek Frontier.*
87. Ralph L. Roys (editor and translator). *The Book of Chilam Balam of Chumayel.*
88. Burr Cartwright Brundage. *Lords of Cuzco: A History and Description of the Inca People in Their Final Days.*
89. John C. Ewers. *Indian Life on the Upper Missouri.*
90. Max L. Moorhead. *The Apache Frontier:* Jacobo Ugarte and Spanish-Indian Relations in Northern New Spain, 1769–1791.
91. France Scholes and Ralph L. Roys. *The Maya Chontal Indians of Acalan-Tixchel.*
92. Miguel León-Portilla. *Pre-Columbian Literatures of Mexico.* Translated by Grace Lobanov and the author.
93. Grace Steele Woodward. *Pocahontas.*
94. Gottfried Hotz. *Eighteenth-Century Skin Paintings.* Translated by Johannes Malthaner.
95. Virgil J. Vogel. *American Indian Medicine.*
96. Bill Vaudrin. *Tanaina Tales from Alaska.* Introduction by Joan B. Townsend.
97. Georgiana C. Nammack. *The Iroquois Land Frontier in the Colonial Period.*
98. Eugene R. Craine and Reginald C. Reindorp (editors and translators). *The Chronicles of Michoacán.*
99. J. Eric S. Thompson. *Maya History and Religion.*
100. Peter J. Powell. *Sweet Medicine:* The Continuing Role of the Sacred Arrows, the Sun Dance, and the

Sacred Buffalo Hat in Northern Cheyenne History. 2 volumes.

101. Karen Daniels Petersen. *Indians Unchained*: Plains Indian Art from Fort Marion.
102. Fray Diego Durán. *The Books of the Gods and Rites and The Ancient Calendar*. Translated and edited by Fernando Horcasitas and Doris Heyden. Foreword by Miguel León-Portilla.
103. Bert Anson. *The Miami Indians*: Sovereigns of the Wabash-Maumee.
104. Robert H. Ruby and John A. Brown. *The Spokane Indians*: Children of the Sun. Foreword by Robert L. Bennett.
105. Virginia Cole Trenholm. *The Arapahoes, Our People*.
106. Angie Debo. *A History of the Indians of the United States*.
107. Herman Grey. *Tales from the Mohaves*.
108. Stephen Dow Beckham. *Requiem for a People*: The Rogue Indians and the Frontiersmen.
109. Arrell M. Gibson. *The Chickasaws*.
110. *Indian Oratory*: Famous Speeches by Noted Indian Chieftains, compiled by W. C. Vanderwerth.
111. *The Sioux of the Rosebud*: A History in Pictures. Photographs by John A. Anderson, text by Henry W. Hamilton and Jean Tyree Hamilton.
112. Howard L. Harrod. *Mission Among the Blackfeet*.
113. Mary Whatley Clarke. *Chief Bowles and the Texas Cherokees*.
114. William E. Unrau. *The Kansa Indians*: A History of the Wind People.
115. Jack D. Forbes. *Apache, Navaho, and Spaniard*.
116. W. David Baird. *Peter Pitchlynn*: Chief of the Choctaws.

117. *Life and Death in Milpa Alta:* A Nahuatl Chronicle of Díaz and Zapata. Translated and edited by Fernando Horcasitas, with a foreword by Miguel León-Portilla.

118. Ralph L. Roys. *The Indian Background of Colonial Yucatán.* With an introduction by J. Eric S. Thompson.

119. *Cry of the Thunderbird:* The American Indian's Own Story. Edited by Charles Hamilton.

120. Robert H. Ruby and John A. Brown. *The Cayuse Indians:* Imperial Tribesmen of Old Oregon.

121. George A. Schultz. *Indian Canaan:* Isaac McCoy and the Vision of an Indian State. Foreword by Robert E. Bell.

122. Hugh A. Dempsey. *Crowfoot:* Chief of the Blackfeet. Foreword by Paul F. Sharp.

123. D. S. Otis. *The Dawes Act and the Allotment of Indian Land.* Edited and with an introduction by Francis Paul Prucha, S.J.